ChatGPT for Java

A Hands-on Developer's Guide to ChatGPT and Open AI APIs

Bruce Hopkins

Foreword by Patricia Thaine,
Co-Founder & CEO, Private AI

Apress®

ChatGPT for Java: A Hands-on Developer's Guide to ChatGPT and Open AI APIs

Bruce Hopkins
Beaverton, OR, USA

ISBN-13 (pbk): 979-8-8688-0115-0   ISBN-13 (electronic): 979-8-8688-0116-7
https://doi.org/10.1007/979-8-8688-0116-7

Managing Director, Apress Media LLC: Welmoed Spahr
Acquisitions Editor: Melissa Duffy
Development Editor: Laura Berendson
Editorial Assistant: Gryffin Winkler

Cover designed by eStudioCalamar

Distributed to the book trade worldwide by Springer Science+Business Media New York, 1 New York Plaza, Suite 4600, New York, NY 10004-1562, USA. Phone 1-800-SPRINGER, fax (201) 348-4505, e-mail orders-ny@springer-sbm.com, or visit www.springeronline.com. Apress Media, LLC is a California LLC and the sole member (owner) is Springer Science + Business Media Finance Inc (SSBM Finance Inc). SSBM Finance Inc is a **Delaware** corporation.

For information on translations, please e-mail booktranslations@springernature.com; for reprint, paperback, or audio rights, please e-mail bookpermissions@springernature.com.

Apress titles may be purchased in bulk for academic, corporate, or promotional use. eBook versions and licenses are also available for most titles. For more information, reference our Print and eBook Bulk Sales web page at http://www.apress.com/bulk-sales.

Any source code or other supplementary material referenced by the author in this book is available to readers on GitHub. For more detailed information, please visit https://www.apress.com/gp/services/source-code.

Paper in this product is recyclable

Table of Contents

About the Author ix

About the Technical Reviewer xi

Foreword xiii

Chapter 1: Introducing ChatGPT for Java Developers..........................1

Who Is This Book For?..1

Chapter Overview...2

Download the Code Now!...2

So, What Exactly Is ChatGPT and Why Do I Need to Use the OpenAI APIs? 2

Regex vs. ChatGPT: Fight! 5

    Analysis Question #1: Who Didn't Get Any Ice Cream and Why? 7

    Analysis Question #2: Which Kid Was Probably Left Sad?............................9

Let's Unlearn Some Words in Order to Learn More About the ChatGPT API 10

    Models. Models? Models!!! 10

    When We Talk About Tokens, Think About the StringTokenizer and
    Not Access Tokens...15

    Temperature Is All About Creativity..16

Getting Started with the OpenAI Playground 17

    1. System..19

    2. User 20

    3. Assistant (Optional)..20

    4. Add Message (Optional)...21

    5. View Code (Optional)...21

6. Model (Optional) 21

7. Temperature (Optional) 22

8. Maximum Length (Optional) 22

Try It Now! Experimenting with the "System" Role............................22

Conclusion 23

Chapter 2: Using ChatGPT As Your Java Pair-Programmer 25

Creating Your First Java ChatGPT App: ListModels.java 26

List Models Endpoint...26

Creating the Request...26

Handling the JSON Response 27

Model (JSON)..27

Chat Endpoint..32

Creating the Request...32

Chat (JSON) 33

Handling the Response..42

Chat Completion (JSON) 43

Wait, How Many Tokens Are in My Prompt?.....................................46

ChatGPT Token Counter 46

Creating the Next Java App: ChatGPTClient.java................................48

Conclusion 56

Chapter 3: Using AI in the Enterprise! Creating a Text Summarizer
for Slack Messages...57

So, What Is Prompt Engineering?..58

Updating ChatGPTClient.java (and Related Classes) with the Builder Pattern 58

ChatGPT Is Here to Take Away Everyone's Jobs (Not Really) 64

Examining a Real World Problem: Customer Support for a Software Company 64

Prompt Engineering 101: Text Summarization 68

    Prompt #1: "tl;dr" 69

    Prompt #2: "Explain This in 3 Sentences or Less" 71

    Prompt #3: "I'm a Manager. Explain to Me What Happened" 72

    Prompt #4: "Give Me Suggestions on Next Steps" 74

    Let's Talk About Real Prompt Engineering 77

Registering a Slack Bot App 77

    Specifying What Your Bot Can (and Can't) Do By Setting the Scope 80

    Confirming Your Settings 82

    Viewing the OAuth and Permissions Page 82

    Installing Your Slack Bot App to Your Workspace 83

    Getting Your Slack Bot (Access) Token 85

    Inviting Your Bot to Your Channel 86

Finding the Channel ID of Your Channel 87

Using Your Slack Bot App to Automatically Grab Messages from a Channel 87

    Setting Up Your Dependencies 87

    Programmatically Reading Messages from Slack with
ChannelReaderSlackBot.java 91

Exercises Left for the Reader 96

Conclusion 97

**Chapter 4: Multimodal AI: Creating a Podcast Visualizer
with Whisper and DALL·E 3 ....99**

Introducing the Whisper Model by OpenAI 102

Features and Limitations of the Whisper Model 105

Transcriptions Endpoint 108

    Creating the Request 108

    Request Body (Multipart Form Data) 109

Creating a Utility App to Split Audio Files: AudioSplitter.java 111

Creating the Audio Transcriber: WhisperClient.java 116

Having a Little Fun and Trying Things Out with a Podcast 122

Going Meta: Prompt Engineering GPT-4 to Write a Prompt for DALL·E............. 126

Create Image Endpoint.. 128

    Creating the Request... 128

    Create Image (JSON) 129

    Handling the Response... 131

    Image (JSON).. 132

Creating the Image Generator: DALLEClient.java 132

DALL·E Prompt Engineering and Best Practices 136

    DALL·E Golden Rule #1: Get Familiar with the Types of Images that
    DALL·E Can Generate... 137

    DALL·E Golden Rule #2: Be Descriptive with What You Want in the
    Foreground and Background... 138

Conclusion 139

Exercises Left for the Reader.. 140

**Chapter 5: Creating an Automated Community Manager Bot with
Discord and Java..141**

Choosing Discord as Your Community Platform.. 142

Creating a More Advanced Bot Than Our Slack Bot 143

Creating a More Advanced Bot Than Any Typical Discord Bot.......................... 143

    Understanding the Roles for the Bots... 144

Our Example Bank: Crook's Bank.. 144

First Things First: Create Your Own Discord Server 145

Create the Q&A Channel... 147

Registering a New Discord Bot App with Discord 148

Specifying General Info for the Bot.. 150

Specifying OAuth2 Parameters for the Bot 151

Invite Your Bot to Your Server.. 153

Getting the Discord ID Token for Your Bot and Setting the Gateway Intents 155

Creating a Q&A Bot App in Java to Answer Questions from a Channel............ 158

    Setting Up Your Dependencies 159

Creating The First Discord Bot: TechSupportBotDumb.java............................. 160

    Loving the Lambda Expression to Simplify Code... 164

    Handling Messages Sent to the Discord Server 165

    Success! Running Your First Discord Bot: TechSupportBotDumb.java........... 166

Streamlining the Process of Registering Our Next Discord Bot App with
Discord.. 167

    Registering a New Discord Bot App with Discord... 167

    Specifying General Info for the Bot.. 168

    Specifying OAuth2 Parameters for the Bot.. 168

    Invite Your Bot to Your Server 169

    Getting the Discord ID Token for Your Bot and Setting the
    Gateway Intents.. 169

Creating the Next Discord Bot: ContentModeratorBotDumb.java 169

    Handling Messages Sent to the Discord Server 173

    Success Again! Running Your Second Discord Bot:
    ContentModeratorBotDumb.java... 174

Conclusion 174

Exercises Left for the Reader.. 175

**Chapter 6: Adding Intelligence to Our Discord Bots, Part 1:
          Using the Chat Endpoint for Q&A....................................177**

Making TechSupportBot.java More Intelligent 178

Important Changes to Note from the Previous Version of the Tech
Support Bot 185

    Updates to the onMessageReceived() Method 186

Analyzing ChatGPTClientForQAandModeration.java 186

    Using JSONPath in Order to Extract Content Quickly in JSON Files 192

    Running Our Intelligent Q&A Bot: TechSupportBot.java 192

We Have a Monumental Achievement... With One Slight Flaw 195

Update the System Message to ChatGPT and Let's Try Again 196

Conclusion 198

Chapter 7: Adding Intelligence to Our Discord Bots, Part 2:
Using the Chat and Moderation Endpoints for
Moderation 199

Moderations Endpoint 201

    Creating the Request 202

    Create Moderation (JSON) 203

    Handling the JSON Response 203

    Moderation (JSON) 204

Creating Our Client for the Moderations Endpoint: ModerationClient.java 208

Making ContentModeratorBot.java More Intelligent 213

Important Changes to Note from the Previous Version of the Content
Moderator Bot 219

    Updates to the onMessageReceived( ) Method 220

Running Our Intelligent Content Moderator Bot: ContentModeratorBot.java 221

Conclusion 223

Exercises Left for the Reader 223

Appendix 1: List of OpenAI Models 225

Index 229

About the Author

Bruce Hopkins is a technical writer and world-renowned expert. He is both an Oracle Java Champion as well as an Intel Software Innovator. Bruce is also the author of the Apress book *Bluetooth for Java*.

About the Technical Reviewer

Van VanArsdale is a technology leader with over 30 years of experience in the software industry. He holds a B.S. in Computer Information Systems from the University of Massachusetts Lowell and an M.S. in CIS from Missouri State University. He has worked as a software engineer, architect, manager, and teacher. Van currently leads a team at a top financial services company and is an adjunct instructor at Missouri State University.

Foreword

Having had the pleasure of knowing Bruce for a few years now, I've witnessed his ability to take cutting-edge concepts and problems and make them accessible to programmers from a myriad of different backgrounds and abilities. Bruce's experience is particularly suitable for the task of breaking down many of the latest AI technologies, like ChatGPT, into core components that developers can use in their day-to-day problem-solving. He is the co-author of *Bluetooth for Java*, which came out just four years after Bluetooth made its way into the market, and he is the author of numerous technical guides written for major technology companies who needed their newest inventions to be adopted by developers.

As the co-founder and CEO of a Microsoft-backed AI company, called Private AI, I have the privilege of speaking with developers, managers, and C-level executives from organizations around the world not only about the implementation of responsible use of data but about the questions they have around generative AI, what kinds of problems to tackle, and where to start. Technology like ChatGPT is so new that the underlying model architecture allowing it to perform as well as it does – the Transformer architecture, that is – only came out in 2017 in the research paper titled "Attention Is All You Need." As a result, a lot of the key questions that managers are struggling with are also questions developers are avidly diving into, including "What can I do with this technology?", "How and where should I implement it?", "Where should I start?", "What are the pitfalls?", and the ever-gnawing question when a lot of attention is placed on new inventions: "Is this all just hype?"

Happily, many of these questions are addressed in concrete ways within this book, which is a crucial step toward cutting through to the core of what a new technology is actually useful for. In the same way that learning a programming language teaches you how to think in a completely different way than when using natural language, learning how to make the best use of AI makes you think in a completely different way than programming. In natural languages, the key is learning vocabulary, grammar, syntax, and semantics. In programming languages, it is logic, mathematics, syntax, scale, and significantly more of a first principles understanding of the world. In Artificial Intelligence, it's all about the data and how they relate to the task at hand. You can have the most powerful models in the world for generating text, for navigating roads, for generating art, but if you apply them to a task they were not meant for, prepare to be disappointed. However, if you understand fundamentally what they were built to do and use them accordingly, prepare to be amazed.

The concise, practical examples in this book will not only allow for you to quickly start building projects with ChatGPT, but will also start honing your intuition around how to think about this technology. Indeed, while the focus is working in Java, developers who use any programming language will benefit from diving in.

Patricia Thaine
Co-Founder and CEO, Private AI
www.private-ai.com

CHAPTER 1

Introducing ChatGPT for Java Developers

Who Is This Book For?

First of all, this book is for Java developers who don't have any training or experience in artificial intelligence, natural language processing, machine learning, or deep learning. You may have heard of the term "language model," but I'm going to assume that it's NOT a term that you use every day.

Secondly, you might be familiar with (or have tried) ChatGPT, but you don't *quite* understand how everything works "under the hood" and you're not sure how to get started in order to use Java and ChatGPT programmatically together to "AI enable" your own applications and services.

Note Although ChatGPT is a household name, OpenAI, the company behind it, lacks broad recognition and isn't as widely recognized. So, although this book is about how to use ChatGPT programmatically within your Java apps, the APIs that we will be using are officially the OpenAI REST APIs. Therefore, we'll be using the term "ChatGPT API" and "OpenAI API" synonymously.

© Bruce Hopkins 2024
B. Hopkins, *ChatGPT for Java*, https://doi.org/10.1007/979-8-8688-0116-7_1

Chapter Overview

In this chapter, we're going to dive right in and explain a few terms that you might not be familiar with, and then go straight to the ChatGPT Playground. The Playground is essentially a web interface for developers that's built on top of ChatGPT REST API. So, once you're familiar with the Playground, the calls and responses from the ChatGPT API will feel like second nature to you.

Download the Code Now!

This book is filled with tons of examples and example code, so why bother typing everything yourself? Below is the URL to the GitHub repo to access the source code.

https://github.com/Apress/ChatGPT-for-Java

So, What Exactly Is ChatGPT and Why Do I Need to Use the OpenAI APIs?

Simply stated, ChatGPT is a group of **language models** (which are the result of training deep learning algorithms) developed by OpenAI that is capable of generating human-like text responses based on given **prompts**. So what's a prompt? A prompt is simply the input text that you give to ChatGPT. So let's kick things off by giving ChatGPT a prompt to ask how well it's familiar with Java design patterns (Listing 1-1).

Listing 1-1. PROMPT. A Simple Prompt with ChatGPT About Java
Design Patterns

```
Describe 3 commonly used design patterns used by Java
developers and why those patterns are important
```

If you've had the opportunity to work at a company using Java
professionally, then you've probably received a question very similar to the
prompt above in an interview. Listing 1-2 is ChatGPT's response.

Listing 1-2. RESPONSE. ChatGPT's Response to the Prompt in
Listing 1-1

```
Certainly! Design patterns are reusable solutions to common
problems that arise in software design. They are best practices
that experienced developers have discovered and refined over
time. Java developers frequently utilize design patterns due to
the language's object-oriented nature. Here are three commonly
used design patterns in Java:

1. Singleton Pattern:
   - Purpose: This pattern ensures that a class has only
one instance and provides a global point of access to that
instance. It's particularly useful when you want to control
access to shared resources, such as configuration managers or
connection pools.
   - Importance: The Singleton pattern is important because it
provides a controlled mechanism to prevent creating multiple
instances of a class, which can save memory and synchronize
access to resources. Moreover, it ensures that operations using
```

3

the singleton are using the same instance and data, which is critical in scenarios where consistent state or coordinated actions are required.

2. Observer Pattern:

  - Purpose: This pattern defines a one-to-many dependency between objects. When one object (known as the subject or observable) changes its state, all of its dependents (observers) are notified and updated automatically. It's the underlying principle behind the Model-View-Controller (MVC) architecture, where the model is the subject and the views are observers.

  - Importance: The Observer pattern is vital for building systems that are modular and decoupled. Changes in one part of the system don't directly affect others, allowing for easier maintenance and scalability. This pattern also makes it easier to add new observers without modifying existing code, enhancing the system's extensibility.

3. Factory Pattern:

  - Purpose: The Factory pattern provides an interface for creating instances of a class, but it's up to the derived subclasses to implement the method and determine which class to instantiate. It promotes the loose coupling by eliminating the need to bind application-specific classes into the code. Instead, the code interacts only with the resulting interface or abstract class, so the system can evolve without altering the calling code.

  - Importance: Using the Factory pattern, a system can be more flexible and scalable. If there's a need to introduce a new product or modify an existing one, it can be done without disturbing the existing code. It encapsulates the object creation process and separates it from the main logic of the program, promoting the Single Responsibility Principle. This ensures that a class is only responsible for one reason to change.

All these patterns, and many more, provide a vocabulary for developers, making it easier to communicate complex software designs and concepts. They embody solutions to recurring problems and can significantly speed up the development process, reduce errors, and improve code quality.

Not bad, huh? ChatGPT was not only able to provide a list of common design patterns used by Java developers, but also explain valid reasons on why they are important – all done in Natural Language.

So, at the end of the day, what does this mean for Java developers? Well, it's actually a big deal. That's because developers are now able to create applications that can have some type of "understanding" of text in Natural Language. Before the advent of AI tools like ChatGPT, developers typically had to create regular expressions (also called "regex") in order to perform rudimentary character and String pattern matching within a body of text. However, pattern matching and Natural Language Understanding are two totally different things.

Regex vs. ChatGPT: Fight!

Note   If you already know that a regular expression can't perform Natural Language Understanding or sentiment analysis, then feel free to skip this section.

I'm thoroughly convinced that every programmer somewhere in their lifetime has met *some guy* who happens to be an expert in writing regular expressions. Regular expressions are great because they serve the purpose of being able to parse large amounts of text in order to find patterns within the text programmatically.

However, one of the biggest downsides to regular expressions is that once they have been written, they are extremely difficult to read (in my opinion, even by the developer who originally wrote it).

So let's see how regex holds up against ChatGPT, which has Natural Language Processing (NLP) and Natural Language Understanding (NLU) capabilities.

Listing 1-3 is a story of an impractically sad situation. However, it drives home the point that although regular expressions can be used to find words and phrases within a body of text, it can't be used to provide any type of NLU.

Listing 1-3. Sadstory.txt - A Sad Story About a Kid Who Didn't Eat Ice Cream

```
In the city of Buttersville,USA on Milkmaid street, there's
a group of three friends: Marion Yogurt, Janelle de Queso,
and Steve Cheeseworth III. On a hot summer's day, they
heard the music from an ice cream truck, and decided to buy
something to eat.

Marion likes strawberries, Janelle prefers chocolate, and Steve
is lactose intolerant. That day, only two kids ate ice cream,
and one of them bought a bottle of room-temperature water. The
ice cream truck was fully stocked with the typical flavors of
ice cream.
```

Analysis Question #1: Who Didn't Get Any Ice Cream and Why?

Now let's analyze this for a bit and ask some questions among ourselves. First of all, who didn't get any ice cream and why? The obvious answer is that Steve did not get any ice cream because of his lactose intolerance. However, since the story did not directly say that Steve did not buy ice cream, there's no way for a regular expression to match a text pattern in the story.

The regular expression could look for keywords such as "didn't have," "no ice cream," or the names of the kids. However, it would only be able to provide a response based on the presence of these patterns. For example, if the regular expression matches the pattern "didn't have" or "no ice cream" with Steve's name, it could show you the result of the text pattern. However, it certainly wouldn't be able to explain **why** Steve was the one who didn't have ice cream or provide any context-specific reasoning.

Now, let's provide the same story to ChatGPT and ask the question, "Who didn't get any ice cream?" Listing 1-4 takes our question and the preceding story and puts both together as a prompt.

Listing 1-4. PROMPT. The Sad Story Put into a Prompt

```
Using the information in the following story, who didn't get
any ice cream and why?
###
In the city of Buttersville,USA on Milkmaid street, there's
a group of three friends: Marion Yogurt, Janelle de Queso,
and Steve Cheeseworth III. On a hot summer's day, they
heard the music from an ice cream truck, and decided to buy
something to eat.
```

```
Marion likes strawberries, Janelle prefers chocolate, and Steve
is lactose intolerant. That day, only two kids ate ice cream,
and one of them bought a bottle of room-temperature water. The
ice cream truck was fully stocked with the typical flavors of
ice cream.
```

Notice how it is a best practice to provide some type of separation, in this case, "###", when creating a prompt (like the one above) where you have both instructions and data together. Later on, when we start using either the Playground or Java to programmatically invoke the ChatGPT API, you'll see that there's a much better way to provide that separation.

So, after sending the prompt, ChatGPT will provide you an answer as shown in Listing 1-5.

Listing 1-5. RESPONSE. ChatGPT's Answer to Analysis Question #1

```
Based on the given information, Steve is lactose intolerant and
therefore cannot eat ice cream. Therefore, Steve is the one who
didn't get any ice cream.
```

As you can see, ChatGPT can utilize NLP and NLU, and therefore it can *understand* (artificially intelligently, that is) the context of the scenario. It can interpret the relationships between the kids, their preferences, and Steve's lactose intolerance. It is able to understand that the last names of the children, the street name, and the city name are the names of dairy products, but are obviously irrelevant to the question at hand.

Analysis Question #2: Which Kid Was Probably Left Sad?

Now, to further prove the point that a regular expression is unable to provide any type of NLP or NLU, now let's use a new term called **sentiment analysis**. Therefore, after the ice cream truck drove away, which kid was left sad?

Since the story had no mention of any of the children's feelings or emotions, there is no text pattern that would allow any regular expression to return a match.

However, if you posed the same question to ChatGPT, it will return a response as shown in Listing 1-6.

Listing 1-6. RESPONSE. ChatGPT's Answer to Analysis Question #2

Since Steve is lactose intolerant and cannot eat ice cream, he would be the kid left sad because he couldn't enjoy the ice cream like Marion and Janelle.

Therefore, ChatGPT is able to comprehend the scenario, reason through the information, and provide a correct answer along with an *explanation* for that answer.

Let's Unlearn Some Words in Order to Learn More About the ChatGPT API

First of all, before you get started working with the ChatGPT and OpenAI APIs, there are few words and terms that you should be familiar with first; otherwise, things won't exactly make sense. So let's make sure that we're all clear on the definition of Models, Prompts, Tokens, and Temperature when using ChatGPT programmatically.

Models. Models? Models!!!

As a Java developer, when you hear the term "model," you may immediately think of object-oriented programming and the representation of real-world entities in your Java class, right? For example, think of the term, "object model." Additionally, if you're ever worked with any type of database before, then the term "model" may ALSO conjure into your mind the idea of the representation of data and their relationships in your database. For example, think of the term, "data model."

However, when working with the ChatGPT APIs (and artificial intelligence in general, for that matter), you need to forget both of those definitions, because they don't apply. In the realm of artificial intelligence, a "model" is a pre-trained **neural network**.

Remember, as I mentioned earlier, you won't need a PhD in Machine Learning in order to read this book. So what's a neural network? Simply stated, a neural network is a fundamental component of artificial intelligence systems, because they are designed to simulate the way the human brain works by using interconnected layers of artificial neurons to process and analyze data. These networks can be trained on vast amounts of data to learn patterns, relationships, and to make predictions.

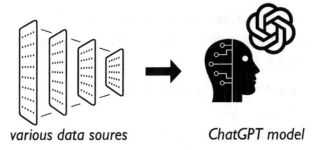

various data soures   *ChatGPT model*

Figure 1-1. *An AI Model Is Trained on Vast Amounts of Data*

In the context of AI, a "pre-trained model" refers to a neural network that has been trained on a specific task or dataset before being made available for use by developers. This training process involves exposing the model to large amounts of labeled and categorized (also called, "annotated") data and adjusting its internal parameters to optimize its performance on the given task.

Let's look at some of the models provided by OpenAI for developers to use to AI-enable their applications.

GPT-4   GPT-4 is the latest generation of OpenAI's GPT set of models. GPT stands for Generative Pre-trained Transformer, and these models have been trained to understand natural language as well as multiple programming languages. The GPT-4 models take text and images as inputs as the prompt and provide text as the output.

Some of the GPT-4 models available are

- gpt-4
- gpt-4-32k
- gpt-4-vision

(*continued*)

11

GPT-3.5   GPT-3.x is the previous generation of OpenAI's GPT set of models. The original ChatGPT released to the public in November 2022 used GPT 3.

Some of the GPT-3 models available are
- `gpt-3.5-turbo`
- `gpt-3.5-turbo-16k`

DALL·E   The DALL·E model can generate and edit images given a natural language prompt.

Later in this book in Chapter 4, we're going to have some fun with the DALL·E model to visualize the conversation of what is being discussed in your favorite podcast episode.

Some of the DALL·E models available are
- `dall-e-3`
- `dall-e-2`

TTS   The TTS model takes text and converts it to audio with surprisingly good results. In most cases, the audio is almost indistinguishable from a human voice.

Some of the TTS models available are
- `tts-1`
- `tts-1-hd`

Whisper   Simply stated, the Whisper model converts audio into text.
In this book, we're going to use the Whisper model to search for text in a podcast episode.

(continued)

Embeddings   The Embeddings model can convert large amounts of text into a numerical representation of how the Strings in the text are related. So how is that useful? Embeddings allows developers to do specific tasks using custom datasets. Yes, this means that you can train the embeddings model on specific data that is relevant to your application. This allows you to do operations such as

- Searching within your own body of text
- Clustering data so that Strings of text are grouped by their similarity
- Getting Recommendations (where items with related text strings are recommended)
- Detecting Anomalies (where outliers with little relatedness are identified)
- Measuring Diversity (where similarity distributions are analyzed)
- Classifying Data (where text strings are classified by their most similar label)

(continued)

13

Moderation	The moderation models are fine-tuned models that can detect whether text may be sensitive or unsafe. These models can analyze text content and classify it according to the following categories:

- Hate
- Hate/threatening
- Harassment
- Harassment/threatening
- Self-harm
- Self-harm/intent
- Self-harm/instructions
- Sexual
- Sexual/minors
- Violence
- Violence/graphic

The moderation models available are
- Text-moderation-latest
- Text-moderation-stable

Legacy and Deprecated	Since the debut of ChatGPT, OpenAI has continued to support their older AI models, but they have been labeled as "legacy" or "deprecated" models. These models continue to exist; however they have released other models that are more accurate, faster, and cheaper to use.

Note   This is by no means an exhaustive list of models available for developers provided by OpenAI! As newer models are released, the older models will be marked as legacy or deprecated. Therefore, it's important to stay up to date by checking the list of available models on the OpenAI documentation list of models:

https://platform.openai.com/docs/models

When We Talk About Tokens, Think About the StringTokenizer and Not Access Tokens

When using a third-party API, you might think of a token in the same sense as an access token, which is typically a UUID that allows you to identify yourself and maintain a session with the service. Well, forget that definition for now.

Now, as a Java developer, you've probably had the opportunity to use the class, `java.util.StringTokenizer`, in order to take a String and split it up into an Array of smaller Strings so that you can iterate over it for whatever purpose you need. For example, if you had a paragraph of text, you could let your delimiter be "." in order to get an Array of sentences in the paragraph.

The good news is that the OpenAI API concept of a **token** is very familiar to the Java concept in the sense that it is a fragment of text. For the OpenAI APIs, a token is a chunk of a text that is approximately 4 characters long. That's it – nothing else special.

So if a token is approximately a 4-character chunk of text, then why do we care about it?

When working with the OpenAI textual models, developers need to be aware of token limitations, because they impact the cost and performance of API calls. For example, the gpt-3.5-turbo model has a token limitation of 4096 tokens, while the gpt-4-vision model has a limitation of 128,000 tokens (which is approximately the size of a 300-page novel). Token limitations for models are called **context windows**.

As a result, developers need to take into account the length of the prompts as inputs and outputs to the models, ensuring that they fit within the model's token constraints.

Table 1-1 provides a list of some of the most current models with the token limitations and their pricing.

Table 1-1. *List of Models with Their Token Limitations and the Cost Per Token*

Model	Max Tokens	Cost of Token Input	Cost of Token Output
gpt-4	8,192	$0.03 / 1K tokens	$0.06 / 1K tokens
gpt-4-32k	32,768	$0.06 / 1K tokens	$0.12 / 1K tokens
gpt-4-vision	128,000	$0.01 / 1K tokens	$0.03 / 1K tokens
gpt-3.5-turbo-instruct	4,096	$0.0015 / 1K tokens	$0.002 / 1K tokens
gpt-3.5-turbo-16k	16,384	$0.0010 / 1K tokens	$0.002 / 1K tokens
text-embedding-ada-002	8192	$0.0001 / 1K tokens	

Temperature Is All About Creativity

Of course, ChatGPT isn't sentient, so it's incapable of thinking as we humans do. However, by adjusting the **temperature** setting in your prompts to the ChatGPT API, you can enable the responses to be more creative. But understanding what *it* understands is crucial if you want to make best use of its potential.

Figure 1-2. *Modify the Temperature in Order to Get More (or Less) Creative Responses*

Getting Started with the OpenAI Playground

Now it's time to take the concepts that we've learned so far and start to put them to good use! However, we need to do first things first, and therefore, you will need to have a developer account with OpenAI and create an API key.

Head over to the following URL to create your dev account and API key:

```
https://platform.openai.com/account/api-keys
```

As you can see from the image in Figure 1-3, you can name your API key anything that you want.

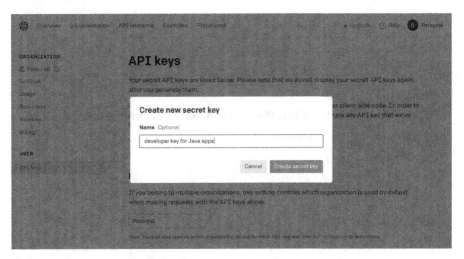

Figure 1-3. *Before You Can Access the Playground or Make API Calls, You Need to Have an API Key*

17

You should be aware that as a requirement to create an API key, you will need to provide to OpenAI a credit card so that you can be billed for usage of their models.

Now that you've got your API key, let's go straight to the Chat Playground at the following URL:

```
https://platform.openai.com/playground
```

Upon entering the Playground, click the combobox at the top and select Chat the option to end the Chat Playground, as shown in Figure 1-4.

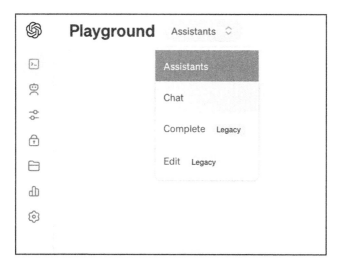

Figure 1-4. *After Entering the Playground, Select the Chat Option*

Figure 1-5 depicts the Chat Playground, with certain parts numbered so that they can be easily identified.

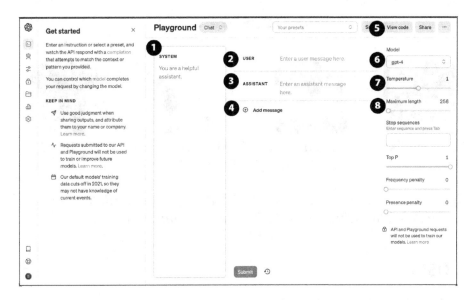

Figure 1-5. *The Chat Playground Can Be a Little Daunting at First Glance*

1. System

As you can see, the user interface for the Chat Playground is vastly more complex than the ChatGPT website that everyone else uses. So let's talk about the **System** field (see Figure 1-5, item 1).

In my opinion, ChatGPT can be described as "a vastly powerful form of artificial intelligence... with amnesia." Therefore, when you're using ChatGPT programmatically, you need to inform the system who it is in the conversation!

Figure 1-6, shown as follows, gives you a glimpse of the thousands of different roles that ChatGPT can play in a conversation.

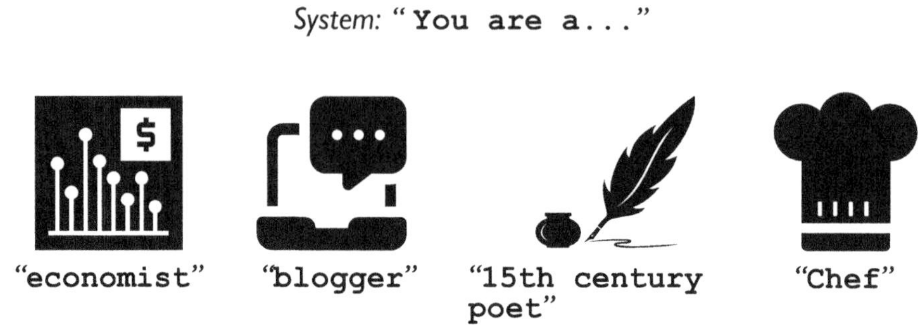

System: "**You are a...**"

"economist"   "blogger"   "15th century   "Chef"
                            poet"

Figure 1-6. *The System Field in the Chat Playground Allows You to Set the Role That ChatGPT Will Play in the Conversation*

2. User

The **User** field (Figure 1-5, item 2) in the ChatGPT Playground is where you type your prompt to ChatGPT, which can be anything that you want, for example, "describe how telemedicine will affect the medical industry."

3. Assistant (Optional)

When you initially load the Chat Playground, the Assistant field (Figure 1-5, item 3) is not visible. In order to make it appear, you need to click the "+" symbol next to "Add Message." Now, you may be asking yourself, "Why is this field needed at all?" Well, that's a fine question. If you want ChatGPT to remember something that it has already told you in a previous conversation, then you need to type into the **Assistant** field anything that it has already told you that you think is relevant in order to continue with the conversation. Remember, it is a vastly powerful AI, but it has amnesia!

4. Add Message (Optional)

The **Add Message** "+" symbol (Figure 1-5, item 4) is where you'd click in order to add either an **Assistant** message to the conversation, or another **User** message. Now, you may ask, "What's the point of adding yet another **User** message to the conversation when I can type what I want in the original **User** field above?" Good question.

If you wanted to separate your command from your data, then you would use a separate **User** message for that.

Do you remember in Listing 1-4 earlier in this chapter, where we had to use the "###" to separate the command to ChatGPT from the data that we wanted it to analyze? Well, this is now no longer needed because the command would be the 1st **User** message, the data would be the 2nd **User** message.

5. View Code (Optional)

After you have submitted your prompt using the playground, you can click the **View code** button (Figure 1-5, item 5) in order to see the code necessary to send the same prompt using any of the languages that they support.

You may notice that Java is not an officially supported language, but we'll fix that in Chapter 2, when we use ChatGPT as a pair programmer and port their REST interface to Java ourselves.

6. Model (Optional)

Earlier in this chapter, we talked about the various models that are available for developers. Click the model field in order to see a list of models that are available.

You may also see that some models have a month and day associated with their name, which is simply a snapshot of that model. Programmatically selecting a snapshot enables developers to have some sort of predictability in the responses that they will receive from ChatGPT, because the current models are always updated.

7. Temperature (Optional)

As noted earlier in this chapter, the temperature selector ranges between 0 and 2 and allows you to select the "randomness" of the response.

8. Maximum Length (Optional)

Do you remember the discussion earlier in this chapter about tokens? By selecting anything in the range for this item, you can adjust the number of tokens (which directly affects the number of words) in the response.

Try It Now! Experimenting with the "System" Role

Now that we're familiar with several of the features of the Chat Playground, let's send our first prompt using the settings discussed above. Listings 1-7 and 1-8 use the same prompt asking ChatGPT to give a few paragraphs on telemedicine, but the role of the system is vastly different from each other.

Listing 1-7. PROMPT. The Pros and Cons of Telemedicine as a Researcher

```
System: You are a strictly factual researcher
User: Write 3 paragraphs on pros and cons of telemedicine
```

Listing 1-8. PROMPT. The Pros and Cons of Telemedicine as an Opinionated Health Blogger

System: You are a highly opinionated health blogger who always has stories with first hand experience
User: Write 3 paragraphs on pros and cons of telemedicine

You are encouraged to try these two prompts yourself and see what the responses are. Adjust the settings for the temperature and token length to get familiar with how those parameters affect the outcome.

Conclusion

You just learned more about how ChatGPT can be used by developers. We covered some of the basics of the Chat Playground, which is a web interface for developers to interact with the ChatGPT API.

We talked about how to set the system, user, and assistant roles in the Chat Playground and how to adjust settings such as the temperature and maximum length of output.

You learned about some of the parameters and terminology necessary to use the Chat Playground, such as the model, the temperature, and tokens. Getting familiar with the parameters of the Chat Playground is essential to knowing how to use the REST API since the Playground is a subset of capabilities offered by the REST API.

In the next chapter, we'll see how to use ChatGPT as your "pair programmer" and port the officially supported ChatGPT REST interface to Java.

CHAPTER 2

Using ChatGPT As Your Java Pair-Programmer

I'm a big fan of some of the practices of XP (eXtreme Programming), and especially pair-programming. No matter what flavor of pair-programming that you prefer, it involves two engineers sitting down at the same screen and solving the same problem together. One of the biggest benefits that you get is a fresh set of eyes on a problem, and of course, you now have two engineers who have "touched" the codebase instead of one. Sometimes you can have one engineer write the code and the other write the tests and the comments. No matter how you slice it, it's all good stuff.

Now, the OpenAI REST APIs for ChatGPT and their other models are officially supported in Python, Typescript, and of course, cURL (which is the de facto standard for REST APIs).

There are a few Java APIs that exist that were created by third-party developers, but the biggest problem (in my opinion) is that this space is rapidly changing. OpenAI is constantly updating both their models and their HTTP interfaces, and as a result, they are adding or deprecating features and functionality frequently. If you choose to use a third-party Java API for your project, you risk the problem of using an API that is outdated or rout of sync with the OpenAI REST API.

© Bruce Hopkins 2024

B. Hopkins, *ChatGPT for Java*, https://doi.org/10.1007/979-8-8688-0116-7_2

So, in this chapter, we're going to use ChatGPT as our pair-programmer and simply port the official OpenAI REST APIs directly to Java. Every time OpenAI makes any changes to their officially supported languages and interfaces, we have everything needed to update our own library instantly. Let's do this!

Creating Your First Java ChatGPT App: `ListModels.java`

We're actually going to accomplish two tasks at once here. We're going to create a basic application in Java using the OpenAI APIs, and in the process, we're going to verify that we've properly obtained an API key. So, needless to say, in case you haven't done so already, follow the instructions in Chapter 1 to create your OpenAI developer account and obtain your API key. Going forward, all the code samples in this book require a valid API key.

List Models Endpoint

One of the most basic (but also essential) services that we can call is the **List Models** endpoint. Why, you may ask? The List Models endpoint allows you to get a list of all the AI models that are currently available for use by developers via the REST API.

Creating the Request

Table 2-1 lists all the HTTP parameters necessary to call the List Models endpoint.

Table 2-1. *The HTTP Parameters Necessary to Call the List Models Endpoint*

HTTP Param	Description
Endpoint URL	https://api.openai.com/v1/models
Method	GET
Header	Authorization: Bearer **$OPENAI_API_KEY**

Handling the JSON Response

After successfully invoking the List Models endpoint, the service will provide a JSON response with the structure shown in Table 2-2.

Model (JSON)

Table 2-2. *The Structure of the Model JSON Object*

Field	Type	Description
object	String	This always returns the literal, "list"
data	Array	A list of AI models offered by OpenAI
↳ id	String	The unique ID of the AI model, which is essentially the full name of the model
↳ object	String	This always returns the literal, "model"
↳ created	integer	The creation date for the model
↳ owned_by	String	The name of the organization that owns the model

(continued)

Table 2-2. (*continued*)

Field	Type	Description
permission	Array	This is an array of metadata for the permissions for the model
root	String	This is typically a copy of the data.id field, which is the model's name
parent	String	This is currently an unused field

Note   Since JSON objects can contain arrays (which can be hard to represent in a table), we're using the notation " ↳ " to indicate the elements of an array. As you can see from the previous table, "id," "object," "created," and "owned_by" are all elements of the "data" array in the JSON response.

Now that we have the details of the HTTP request and response, we can now create the ListModel.java app using the prompt shown in Listing 2-1.

Listing 2-1. PROMPT. Using ChatGPT to Create the ListModels. java App

```
System: You are a Java developer
User: Take the following cURL command and convert it to Java.
Name the file, "ListModels.java"
User: curl https://api.openai.com/v1/models \
  -H "Authorization: Bearer $OPENAI_API_KEY"
```

So, after sending the prompt, ChatGPT will provide you an answer as shown in Listing 2-2.

Listing 2-2. RESPONSE. ListModels.java

```java
import java.io.BufferedReader;
import java.io.InputStreamReader;
import java.net.HttpURLConnection;
import java.net.URL;

public class ListModels {
        public static void main(String[] args) {
        try {
            // Create URL object for the API endpoint
            URL url = new URL("https://api.openai.com/v1/
            models");

            // Create HttpURLConnection object
            HttpURLConnection conn = (HttpURLConnection) url.
            openConnection();

            // Set request method
            conn.setRequestMethod("GET");

            // Set Authorization header
            conn.setRequestProperty("Authorization", "Bearer
            $OPENAI_API_KEY");

            // Get response code
            int responseCode = conn.getResponseCode();

            // If the request was successful (status code 200)
            if (responseCode == HttpURLConnection.HTTP_OK) {
                // Read the response from the API
                BufferedReader in = new BufferedReader(new
                InputStreamReader(conn.getInputStream()));
```

```java
        String inputLine;
        StringBuilder response = new StringBuilder();
        while ((inputLine = in.readLine()) != null) {
        response.append(inputLine);
        }
        in.close();

        // Print the response
        System.out.println(response.toString());
    } else {
        System.out.println("Request failed. Response
        Code: " + responseCode);
    }

    // Close the connection
    conn.disconnect();
} catch (Exception e) {
    e.printStackTrace();
}
}

}
```

Fantastic! Now all you have to do is to replace "$OPENAI_API_KEY" with the value of your actual API key.

After running this class, you'll get a JSON file that contains all the models offered by OpenAI's API, as shown in Listing 2-3.

Listing 2-3. RESPONSE. The Partial JSON Response After Running ListModels.java

```
{
```

```json
"object": "list",
"data": [
  {
    "id": "text-search-babbage-doc-001",
    "object": "model",
    "created": 1651172509,
    "owned_by": "openai-dev"
  },
  {
    "id": "gpt-4",
    "object": "model",
    "created": 1687882411,
    "owned_by": "openai"
  },
  {
    "id": "gpt-3.5-turbo-16k",
    "object": "model",
    "created": 1683758102,
    "owned_by": "openai-internal"
  },
  {
    "id": "curie-search-query",
    "object": "model",
    "created": 1651172509,
    "owned_by": "openai-dev"
  },
  {
    "id": "text-davinci-003",
    "object": "model",
    "created": 1669599635,
    "owned_by": "openai-internal"
  },
```

```json
{
  "id": "text-search-babbage-query-001",
  "object": "model",
  "created": 1651172509,
  "owned_by": "openai-dev"
},
{
  "id": "babbage",
  "object": "model",
  "created": 1649358449,
  "owned_by": "openai"
},
...
```

Listing 2-3 is a partial list due to the sheer size of the number of models available for developers to use! The good news, however, is that the full response is provided as a table in the Appendix.

Now that we can programmatically get a list of models available to use, it's time to send prompts to ChatGPT using Java. This is accomplished using the Chat Endpoint.

Chat Endpoint

The Chat Endpoint (formerly called, "Chat Completion") is a REST service that's basically a 1-to-1 representation of what you can do in the Chat Playground; therefore, this service should feel like second nature to you.

Creating the Request

Table 2-3 lists all the HTTP parameters necessary to call the Chat Endpoint.

Table 2-3. *The HTTP Parameters for the Chat Endpoint*

HTTP Param	Description
Endpoint URL	https://api.openai.com/v1/chat/completions
Method	POST
Header	Authorization: Bearer **$OPENAI_API_KEY**
Content-Type	application/json

Table 2-4 describes the format of the JSON object necessary for the request body for the Chat Endpoint. After a quick glance, you can see that only a few fields are actually required in order to successfully invoke the service.

Chat (JSON)

Table 2-4. *The Structure of the Chat JSON Object*

Field	Type	Required?	Description
model	String	Required	The ID of the model you want to use for Chat Completion. Compatible models include • gpt-4 • gpt-4-0613 • gpt-4-32k • gpt-4-32k-0613 • gpt-3.5-turbo • gpt-3.5-turbo-0613 • gpt-3.5-turbo-16k • gpt-3.5-turbo-16k-0613

(continued)

Table 2-4. (*continued*)

Field	Type	Required?	Description
messages	Array	Required	An array of messages that are a part of the ongoing conversation.
			Each message in the array has two properties: "role" and "content."
↳ role	String	Required	Specifies the role of the message, which can be any of the following: • "system" • "user" • "assistant" • "tool"
↳ content	String	Required	Contains the text of the message for the specified role.
tools	Array	Optional	This allows you to specify a list of tools that the model can call. Currently, the only supported type of tool is a function.
			This parameter enables you to define a set of functions for which the model can generate JSON inputs.

(*continued*)

Table 2-4. (*continued*)

Field	Type	Required?	Description
↳ type	String	Required	This is type of the tool, which can be any of the following: • "function"
↳ function	Array	Optional	An array of functions that the model may use to call in the Chat Completion.
↳↳ name	String	Required	The name of the function to be called. Valid names must be a-z, A-Z, 0-9, or contain underscores and dashes. The maximum length is 64 characters.
↳↳ description	String	Optional	A description of what the function does. This helps the model to decide whether to call the function in the Chat Completion.
↳↳ parameters	JSON object	Required	The parameters the function accepts in the format of a JSON Schema object.

(*continued*)

Table 2-4. (*continued*)

Field	Type	Required?	Description
tool_choice	String or JSON object default: "none" when no functions are included in the request "auto" when functions are included in the request	Optional	This allows you to determine which, if any, function the model should invoke. When set to "none," the model will refrain from calling any function and will solely generate a message response. When set to "auto," the model has the flexibility to choose between generating a message response or invoking a function based on its internal decision-making process.
temperature	Number or null default: 1	Optional	Valid values range between 0 and 2. Controls the randomness of the model's output. The best practice is to adjust the top_p or temperature, but not both.

(*continued*)

Table 2-4. (*continued*)

Field	Type	Required?	Description
top_p	Number or null	Optional	Valid values range between 0 and 1.
	default: 1		Indicates whether to consider few possibilities (0) or all possibilities (1).
			The best practice is to adjust the top_p or temperature, but not both.
n	integer or null default: 1	Optional	Specifies how many Chat Completion choices the model should generate for each input message.
stream	Boolean or null default: false	Optional	If "stream" is set to "true," partial message updates will be sent as server-sent events.
			This means tokens will be sent as data-only events as they become available, and the stream will end with a "data: [DONE]" message

(*continued*)

Table 2-4. (*continued*)

Field	Type	Required?	Description
stop	String / array / null default: null	Optional	You can provide up to 4 sequences where the API should stop generating further tokens. This can be useful for controlling the length or content of responses.
max_tokens	integer or null default: inf	Optional	This parameter sets the maximum number of tokens that the generated Chat Completion can have.
response_ format	JSON object	Optional	You have two options: { "type": "json_object" } for a JSON object response or { "type": "text" } for a text response

(*continued*)

Table 2-4. (*continued*)

Field	Type	Required?	Description
seed	integer or null	Optional	By specifying a seed, the system will make an attempt to generate repeatable results.
			In theory, this means that if you make repeated requests with the same seed and parameters, you should expect to receive the same result.
			In order to get the seed value to put in the subsequent request, copy the system_fingerprint from your last response.
presence_ penalty	Number or null default: 0	Optional	A number between -2.0 and 2.0.
			Positive values penalize new tokens based on whether they appear in the conversation history, encouraging the model to talk about new topics.

(*continued*)

Table 2-4. (*continued*)

Field	Type	Required?	Description
frequency_ penalty	Number or null defaults: 0	Optional	A number between -2.0 and 2.0. Positive values penalize tokens based on their existing frequency in the conversation history, reducing the likelihood of repeating the same lines verbatim.
logit_bias	JSON Map default: null	Optional	Allows you to modify the likelihood of specific tokens appearing in the completion. You provide a JSON object that maps tokens (specified by their token ID in the tokenizer) to associated bias values from -100 to 100. This bias is added to the model's logits before sampling.
user	String	Optional	This is a unique ID that you can optionally generate to represent your end user. This will help OpenAI monitor and detect abuse.

Note   In this book, we're going to be working with the "stream" parameter set to its default setting, which is false. This means that we are going to receive the results from ChatGPT all at once as a single HTTP response.

However, there are cases where you would want this setting to be set true. Let's say that you're building, for example, an interactive voice-enabled chat bot. Let's also say that you're interested in converting the text from ChatGPT to audio so that your users can hear an audible response. In such a case, then you'd definitely want to set the "stream" parameter to be true. Why is this so? When the response is streamed back to your Java application, you have the opportunity at that moment to convert the text snippet to audio. This will enable you to work in parallel with converting text snippets to audio while receiving more text simultaneously. This will make the response seem more natural to the end user and help the conversation feel like an **actual** conversation.

Listing 2-4 is an example of what the JSON object would look like in order to properly invoke the Chat Endpoint.

Listing 2-4. Example of the Chat JSON Object

```
{
  "model": "gpt-3.5-turbo",
  "messages": [
    {
```

```
      "role": "system",
      "content": "You are a product marketer"
    },
    {
      "role": "user",
      "content": "Explain why Java is so widely used in the
      enterprise "
    }
  ],
  "temperature": 1,
  "max_tokens": 256,
  "top_p": 1,
  "frequency_penalty": 0,
  "presence_penalty": 0
}
```

Handling the Response

After successfully invoking the Chat Endpoint, the API will respond with a Chat Completion object or a stream of completion chunks if streaming is enabled. Here's a breakdown of the Chat Completion object.

Chat Completion (JSON)

Table 2-5. *The Structure of the Chat Competion JSON Object*

Field	Type	Description
id	String	The unique identifier for the Chat Completion.
object	String	This always returns the literal, "chat.completion."
system_ fingerprint	String	Use this parameter as the "seed" in a subsequent request if you want to reproducible results in from a previous conversation.
created	integer	The timestamp of the Chat Completion.
model	String	The model used for the Chat Completion.
choices	Array	A list of Chat Completion choices available.
		You can get more than one choice of messages if you specify the desired number of responses you want with the "n" parameter in the Chat JSON request. See Table 2-4.
↳ index	integer	The index of the choice in the list.
↳ message	Array	A chat completion message generated by the model.

(continued)

Table 2-5. (*continued*)

Field	Type	Description
↳ finish_reason	String	Every response will include a finish_reason. The possible values for finish_reason are
		stop: The API returned complete message, or a message terminated by one of the stop sequences provided via the stop parameter.
		length: The model output was incomplete due to the max_tokens parameter in the request or token limit of the model itself.
		tool_call: The model called a tool, such as a fucntion.
		content_filter: The response was terminated due to a violation of the content filters.
		null: The API response still in progress or incomplete.
usage	Array	Usage statistics for the completion request, including the number of tokens in the prompt, completion, and total request.

(*continued*)

Table 2-5. (*continued*)

Field	Type	Description
↳ prompt_tokens	integer	The number of tokens used in the prompt.
↳ completion_tokens	integer	The number of tokens used in the response.
↳ total_tokens	integer	The sum total of all token in the request and response.

Listing 2-5 is an example of the JSON response after invoking the Chat Endpoint.

Listing 2-5. The Chat Completion JSON Object

```
{
  "id": "chatcmpl-7wUOFQ3S34scDLmrLdWTTqvHmXztQ",
  "object": "chat.completion",
  "created": 1694174199,
  "model": "gpt-3.5-turbo-0613",
  "choices": [
    {
      "index": 0,
      "message": {
        "role": "assistant",
        "content": "Java is widely used in the enterprise
because it is platform-independent, allowing applications to
run on any system. Additionally, Java has a large and mature
```

```
ecosystem with a vast array of libraries, frameworks, and
tools, making it easier for developers to build robust and
scalable enterprise applications."
      },
      "finish_reason": "stop"
    }
  ],
  "usage": {
    "prompt_tokens": 32,
    "completion_tokens": 55,
    "total_tokens": 87
  }
}
```

Wait, How Many Tokens Are in My Prompt?

At a certain point, you're going to start thinking about the prompts that you plan to send to ChatGPT and give considerable thought to the token limitations (and the costs) regarding the model that you want to use. In case you forgot, be sure to refer back to Table 1-1 for a list of models and the price of the tokens. Additionally, OpenAI created a simple to use website that allows you to see how many tokens are in your prompt, as shown in Figure 2-1.

ChatGPT Token Counter

```
https://platform.openai.com/tokenizer
```

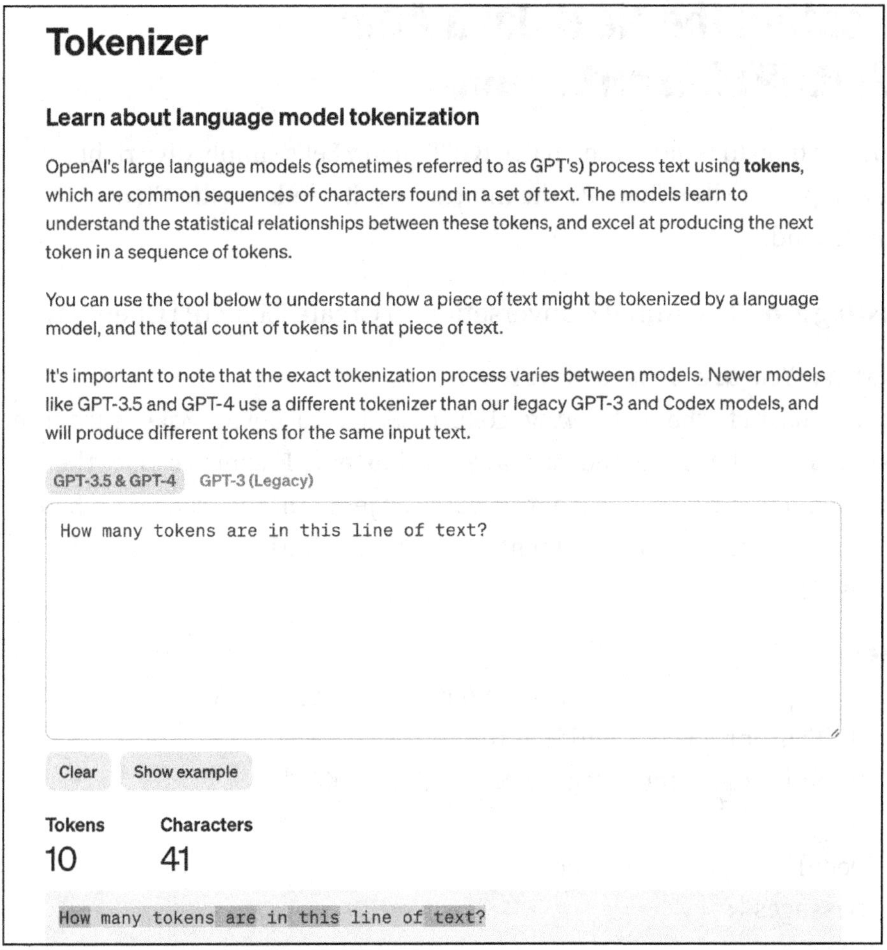

Tokenizer

Learn about language model tokenization

OpenAI's large language models (sometimes referred to as GPT's) process text using **tokens**, which are common sequences of characters found in a set of text. The models learn to understand the statistical relationships between these tokens, and excel at producing the next token in a sequence of tokens.

You can use the tool below to understand how a piece of text might be tokenized by a language model, and the total count of tokens in that piece of text.

It's important to note that the exact tokenization process varies between models. Newer models like GPT-3.5 and GPT-4 use a different tokenizer than our legacy GPT-3 and Codex models, and will produce different tokens for the same input text.

GPT-3.5 & GPT-4   GPT-3 (Legacy)

```
How many tokens are in this line of text?
```

Clear   Show example

Tokens   **Characters**
10   41

How many tokens are in this line of text?

Figure 2-1. *The ChatGPT Tokenizer Can Give You a Quick Count of the Tokens in Your Prompt*

Creating the Next Java App: `ChatGPTClient.java`

Now it's time to build our own ChatGPTClient. Let's simply dive right in, and provide the ChatGPT the information it needs via the ChatGPT Playground.

Listing 2-6. The Initial Conversation to Create ChatGPTClient.java

System: You are a Java developer

User: Convert the following cURL command to Java. Make sure the URL and API keys to the API are variables. I want to use the Jackson library to create the JSON object in the request. Name the main class, ChatGPTClient, and create helper classes if necessary.

User:
```
curl https://api.openai.com/v1/chat/completions \
  -H "Content-Type: application/json" \
  -H "Authorization: Bearer $OPENAI_API_KEY" \
  -d '{
  "model": "gpt-3.5-turbo",
  "messages": [
    {
      "role": "system",
      "content": "You are a product marketer"
    },
    {
      "role": "user",
      "content": "Explain why Java is so widely used in the
      enterprise "
    }
```

```
  ],
  "temperature": 1,
  "max_tokens": 256,
  "top_p": 1,
  "frequency_penalty": 0,
  "presence_penalty": 0
}'
```

The response from ChatGPT was a good start, but didn't have everything exactly as I wanted it. Now, since I didn't specify exactly how the HTTP calls should have been made, ChatGPT decided to use the Apache HTTPClient library. Therefore, I added the following User message (Listing 2-7).

Listing 2-7. PROMPT. Adding Additional Information to the Conversation to Create ChatGPTClient.java

User: I have a Java 11 environment, so use Java 11 HTTP classes for the API calls. I'd rather use pure Java instead of Apache HttpClient

The goal here is to have a conversation. It's impractical to expect ChatGPT to produce exactly what you want in a single prompt. Even developers don't do that! Therefore, feel free to have the conversation with ChatGPT, and clarify to it things that it may have guessed or assumed incorrectly.

Listing 2-8 shows the final result for ChatGPTClient.java.

Listing 2-8. RESPONSE. ChatGPTClient.java

```java
import com.fasterxml.jackson.core.JsonProcessingException;
import com.fasterxml.jackson.databind.ObjectMapper;
import com.fasterxml.jackson.annotation.JsonProperty;

import java.io.BufferedReader;
import java.io.IOException;
import java.io.InputStreamReader;
import java.io.OutputStream;
import java.net.HttpURLConnection;
import java.net.URL;
import java.util.ArrayList;
import java.util.List;

public class ChatGPTClient {

        public static void main(String[] args) {
        String openAIKey = "insert your API key here";
        String endpoint = "https://api.openai.com/v1/chat/
        completions";
        String model = "gpt-3.5-turbo";
        float temperature = 1.0f;
        int max_tokens = 256;
        float top_p = 1.0f;
        int frequency_penalty = 0;
        int presence_penalty = 0;

        List<Message> messages = new ArrayList<>();
        messages.add(new Message("system", "You are a product
        marketer."));
```

```java
messages.add(new Message("user", "Explain why Java is
so widely used in the enterprise"));

String jsonInput = null;
try {
    ObjectMapper mapper = new ObjectMapper();
    Chat chat = new Chat(model, messages, temperature,
    max_tokens, top_p, frequency_penalty, presence_
    penalty);
    jsonInput = mapper.writeValueAsString(chat);
} catch (JsonProcessingException e) {
    e.printStackTrace();
}

try {
    URL url = new URL(endpoint);
    HttpURLConnection connection = (HttpURLConnection)
    url.openConnection();
    connection.setRequestMethod("POST");
    connection.setRequestProperty("Content-Type",
    "application/json");
    connection.setRequestProperty("Authorization",
    "Bearer " + openAIKey);
    connection.setDoOutput(true);

    OutputStream outputStream = connection.
    getOutputStream();
    outputStream.write(jsonInput.getBytes());
    outputStream.flush();
    outputStream.close();

    int responseCode = connection.getResponseCode();
    if (responseCode == HttpURLConnection.HTTP_OK) {
```

```java
                BufferedReader reader = new BufferedReader(new
                InputStreamReader(connection.
                getInputStream()));
                StringBuilder response = new StringBuilder();
                String line;
                while ((line = reader.readLine()) != null) {
                    response.append(line);
                }
                reader.close();

                // Print the response
                System.out.println(response.toString());
            } else {
                System.out.println("Error: " + responseCode);
            }
            connection.disconnect();
        } catch (IOException e) {
            e.printStackTrace();
        }
    }
}

// Helper class to represent the Chat object
static class Chat {

    @JsonProperty("model")
    private String model;

    @JsonProperty("messages")
    private List<Message> messages;

    @JsonProperty("temperature")
    private float temperature;

    @JsonProperty("max_tokens")
```

```java
    private int max_tokens;

    @JsonProperty("top_p")
    private float top_p;

    @JsonProperty("frequency_penalty")
    private int frequency_penalty;

    @JsonProperty("presence_penalty")
    private int presence_penalty;

    public Chat(String model, List<Message> messages,
    float temperature, int max_tokens, float top_p, int
    frequency_penalty, int presence_penalty) {
        this.model = model;
        this.messages = messages;
        this.temperature = temperature;
        this.max_tokens = max_tokens;
        this.top_p = top_p;
        this.frequency_penalty = frequency_penalty;
        this.presence_penalty = presence_penalty;

    }

    // Getters and setters (optional, but can be useful if
        you need to modify the object later)
    }
// Helper class to represent the Chat Message
static class Message {
    @JsonProperty("role")
    private String role;

    @JsonProperty("content")
    private String content;
```

```java
        public Message(String role, String content) {
            this.role = role;
            this.content = content;
        }
    }
}
```

As you examine the preceding code listing, you see that the HTTP calls are done using pure Java APIs and not using any external libraries – just like I requested in the prompt. Note, however, that creating and parsing JSON objects in pure Java can be a pain, so I personally specified that the Jackson API should be used, which (as you can see) is reflected in the imports statements and the code itself.

The resulting code includes two inner classes, Chat and Message, which can easily be separated into separate Java files. I can either do that manually myself, or add a new "User" message to ChatGPT to request the inner classes to be separated into distinct Java files.

After executing ChatGPTClient.java, Listing 2-9 has the response.

Listing 2-9. RESPONSE. The Results from Calling ChatGPTClient.java

```json
{
  "id": "chatcmpl-7xIRvjByGobmWH9Vo7OObHCSSwzgI",
  "object": "chat.completion",
  "created": 1694366627,
  "model": "gpt-3.5-turbo-0613",
  "choices": [
    {
```

```
  "index": 0,
  "message": {
    "role": "assistant",
    "content": "Java is widely used in the enterprise
```
primarily due to its numerous benefits and features that make
it a popular choice among large organizations. Here are some
key reasons why Java is so widely adopted in the enterprise:\n\
n1. Platform Independence: One of the biggest advantages of
Java is its platform independence. Java programs can run on
any operating system, making it highly adaptable across a
wide range of devices and platforms. This makes it easier
for enterprises to develop applications that can be deployed
on different systems without any major modifications.\n\n2.
Robustness and Stability: Java is known for its strong emphasis
on reliability, stability, and error handling. It has a built-
in memory management system that prevents memory leaks and
ensures robust performance. This stability is highly valued in
enterprise environments where systems need to run consistently
without disruptions.\n\n3. Scalability: Java offers excellent
scalability, making it suitable for large-scale enterprise
applications. It provides robust support for multi-threading,
allowing applications to handle a large number of concurrent
users smoothly. Java's ability to handle high traffic loads and
distribute processing across multiple servers makes it ideal
for enterprise-level systems.\n\n4. Rich Standard Library and
Frameworks: Java comes with a comprehensive standard library,
offering a wide range of pre-built functions and classes that
simplify development. Additionally, Java has a"
```
  },
  "finish_reason": "length"
}
```

```
  ],
  "usage": {
    "prompt_tokens": 28,
    "completion_tokens": 256,
    "total_tokens": 284
  }
}
```

Did you notice in the preceding listing that the answer to my prompt was truncated? "Additionally, Java has a" is not a full sentence, but since I requested that no more than 256 tokens should be used in the response, it didn't go beyond that limitation.

Conclusion

Contrary to popular belief, ChatGPT is not a mind-reader! It doesn't have the ability to replace developers and architects because it's (gasp!) artificially intelligent. It's very useful to ask a single question and receive an immediate, straightforward response. It definitely can be used to convert a natural language prompt (or request) into code, but you definitely need a developer to make the judgment call if the resulting code should be used, refined, or completely disregarded.

CHAPTER 3

Using AI in the Enterprise! Creating a Text Summarizer for Slack Messages

In today's corporate world, it's extremely common for companies to have an instance of Slack (or Microsoft Teams) to organize themselves, and use it as a central place of communication to everyone in the company. Now, if you've ever used Slack before, I think you know how easily a channel can become flooded with a ton of messages because **SOME** important thing happened **SOMEWHERE** in the company or the world.

Of course, the more responsibility that you have within the company (i.e., manager, team leader, architect, etc.), the more channels you're expected to participate in. In my opinion, Slack is a double-edged sword. You need to use it to do your job, but as a developer, you definitely can't attend a daily standup meeting and say, "Yesterday, uh, I spent all day reading Slack. No roadblocks."

Additionally, if you work for a company with clients in various time zones (which is quite common nowadays) it's pretty daunting to open Slack in the morning and see a ton of messages that were posted while you were away from the keyboard.

© Bruce Hopkins 2024
B. Hopkins, *ChatGPT for Java*, https://doi.org/10.1007/979-8-8688-0116-7_3

So, in this chapter, we're going to apply AI in the enterprise to make Slack more useful. We'll leverage the code in the previous chapter and create a Slack bot in Java that will summarize the important conversations in a Slack channel. We're going to be utilizing ChatGPT's capabilities for text summarization and focus a bit more on **Prompt Engineering**.

So, What Is Prompt Engineering?

Simply stated, Prompt Engineering is the process of carefully crafting and refining prompts and input parameters to instruct and guide the behavior of ChatGPT and other AI models. It's basically the industry-wide term for creating the right input in order to get the result that you're looking for.

However, before we can continue, let's do a little housekeeping and improve our ChatGPTClient.java from the previous chapter.

Updating ChatGPTClient.java (and Related Classes) with the Builder Pattern

So, in the previous chapter, we created ChatGPTClient.java as a basic app to send our prompts to the Chat Endpoint. It was a good start, but there was definitely some room for improvement.

Let's first look at the constructor for the Chat object, which models the JSON Chat object that is sent to the Chat Endpoint as seen in Listing 3-1.

Listing 3-1. The Constructor for the Chat Object

```
public Chat(String model, List<Message> messages, float
temperature,
            int max_tokens, float top_p, int frequency_
            penalty,
            int presence_penalty) {
```

```
    this.model = model;
    this.messages = messages;
    this.temperature = temperature;
    this.max_tokens = max_tokens;
    this.top_p = top_p;
    this.frequency_penalty = frequency_penalty;
    this.presence_penalty = presence_penalty;
}
```

So, if you refer back to Table 2-4 in Chapter 2, you see that only the
model and messages parameters are actually required to successfully
invoke the Chat Endpoint. All the other parameters are optional, and some
of them have their own built-in defaults if you don't specify anything.
Those are the reasons why we didn't need to "model out" the entire Chat
JSON object.

So, this constructor is basically begging to be refactored using the
Builder Pattern. The Builder Pattern allows us to get an instance of the
object that we want, while ONLY specifying the parameters that we
care about.

Additionally, it makes sense that the Chat and Message objects are no
longer inner classes, and exist in their own .java files. Listing 3-2 shows
how we can get an instance of the Chat object which has been modified
using the Builder Pattern.

Listing 3-2. Getting an Instance of the Chat Object

```
Chat chat = Chat.builder()
    .model(model)
    .messages(messages)
    .temperature(temperature)
    .maxTokens(max_tokens)
    .topP(top_p)
    .frequencyPenalty(frequency_penalty)
```

```
    .presencePenalty(presence_penalty)
    .build();
```

Since the request to the Chat Endpoint MUST has a model and message specified in the Chat JSON object, some defaults have been added to the Chat.java class in order to make it safer to use (safer in the sense of being less error prone to users of the class). Listing 3-3 is the new Chat.java file.

Listing 3-3. Chat.java Now Using the Builder Pattern

```java
import java.util.List;
import java.util.ArrayList;
import com.fasterxml.jackson.annotation.JsonProperty;

public class Chat {
    @JsonProperty("model")
    private String model;

    @JsonProperty("messages")
    private List<Message> messages;

    @JsonProperty("temperature")
    private float temperature;

    @JsonProperty("max_tokens")
    private int max_tokens;

    @JsonProperty("top_p")
    private float top_p;

    @JsonProperty("frequency_penalty")
    private int frequency_penalty;

    @JsonProperty("presence_penalty")
    private int presence_penalty;
```

```java
private Chat(ChatBuilder builder) {
    this.model = builder.model;
    this.messages = builder.messages;
    this.temperature = builder.temperature;
    this.max_tokens = builder.max_tokens;
    this.top_p = builder.top_p;
    this.frequency_penalty = builder.frequency_penalty;
    this.presence_penalty = builder.presence_penalty;
}

public static ChatBuilder builder() {

    // we need a default message here to avoid 400 errors
        from the API
    List<Message> messages = new ArrayList<>();
    messages.add(new Message("system", "You are a helpful
    assistant"));
    messages.add(new Message("user", "hello"));

    return new ChatBuilder().messages(messages);
}

public static class ChatBuilder {
    private String model = "gpt-3.5-turbo";
    private List<Message> messages = null;
    private float temperature = 1.0f;
    private int max_tokens = 2048;
    private float top_p = 0f;
    private int frequency_penalty = 0;
    private int presence_penalty = 0;

    private ChatBuilder() {

    }
```

```java
    public ChatBuilder model(String model) {
        this.model = model;
        return this;
    }

    public ChatBuilder messages(List<Message> messages) {
        this.messages = messages;
        return this;
    }

    public ChatBuilder temperature(float temperature) {
        this.temperature = temperature;
        return this;
    }

    public ChatBuilder maxTokens(int max_tokens) {
        this.max_tokens = max_tokens;
        return this;
    }

    public ChatBuilder topP(float top_p) {
        this.top_p = top_p;
        return this;
    }

    public ChatBuilder frequencyPenalty(int frequency_
    penalty) {
        this.frequency_penalty = frequency_penalty;
        return this;
    }

    public ChatBuilder presencePenalty(int presence_
    penalty) {
        this.presence_penalty = presence_penalty;
```

```
        return this;
    }

    public Chat build() {
        return new Chat(this);
    }

    }
}
```

This class (with this design pattern) is flexible enough for you to add or remove parameters that you need to invoke the Chat Endpoint. If at any time OpenAI adds new parameters and features to the Chat Endpoint, you can modify this class to support the new requirements.

For completeness, Listing 3-4 shows the Message.java class.

Listing 3-4. Message.java

```
import com.fasterxml.jackson.annotation.JsonProperty;

public class Message {
    @JsonProperty("role")
    private String role;

    @JsonProperty("content")
    private String content;

    public Message(String role, String content) {
        this.role = role;
        this.content = content;
    }
}
```

ChatGPT Is Here to Take Away Everyone's Jobs (Not Really)

It is my humble opinion that every company in the world is sitting on a gold mine of untapped information. If you are using any system that keeps a log of exchanges between employees, a database of support requests from your customers, or any large repository of text (yes, this includes your email, Microsoft Exchange, and corporate Gmail), then you have a large repository of unstructured text that is waiting to be utilized.

Therefore, the best use of ChatGPT is not to eliminate anyone's jobs. It should be used in order to augment and extend what team members in your company are already doing. As we saw in the previous chapter, as a programmer, ChatGPT can work as a very effective Pair-Programmer. It is also very good at performing certain difficult tasks very efficiently and quickly. So, let's see a practical example of what can be done in order to make useful a large source of unstructured text.

Examining a Real World Problem: Customer Support for a Software Company

One of the most grueling tasks in software development is providing tech support. Imagine the joys of fielding calls and messages all day from people who might be frustrated, confused, or just in need of a solution while using your software. Here's some of the reasons why customer support is a tough nut to crack:

- Your end users and your customers are notoriously bad at explaining problems with your software.

- Level 1 technicians, often the first line of defense, typically handle the most basic issues or user errors. But when problems get more complex, users are escalated to Level 2.

- The mid-tier is a tricky place, because they have more
knowledge and experience than the tech support staff
at Level 1; however, they don't have the opportunity to
directly get answers from the end user.

- Really bad problems get escalated to Level 3; however,
these are the most expensive tech support staff because
they have the most knowledge and experience. They
have hands-on experience with the code as well as the
servers and the infrastructure.

So let's work with a real world example of a typical conversation within
a typical tech support channel within Slack. Below is a list of the team
members and their roles within a fictional company:

- Fatima (Customer Service Representative)

- John (Software Engineer)

- Dave (PM)

- Keith (CTO)

Listing 3-5 provides an example of a conversation between the
team members at a software startup. Fatima, the customer service
representative, lets the team know that their app is crashing immediately
after launching (not a good problem to have). Keith, the CTO, steps in
immediately to escalate the issue.

Listing 3-5. Team Members Within a Slack Channel Trying to
Analyze a Customer's Problem

```
Fatima [16:00 | 02/08/2019]: Hey everyone, I have an urgent
issue to discuss. I just got off a call with a client who's
experiencing app crashes as soon as they load it. They're
really frustrated. Can we get this sorted ASAP? 😣
```

Keith [16:01 | 02/08/2019]: Thanks for bringing this to our attention, Fatima. Let's jump on this right away. @John, can you take the lead in investigating the issue since our architect is out sick today?

John [16:02 | 02/08/2019]: Sure thing, Keith. I'll dive into the codebase and see if I can find any potential culprits for the crashes.

John [16:02 | 02/08/2019]: Fatima, could you gather some additional information from the client? Ask them about the specific device, operating system, and any recent updates they might have installed.

Fatima [16:03 | 02/08/2019]: Absolutely, John. I'll reach out to the client immediately and gather those details. Will update you all once I have them.

Dave [16:04 | 02/08/2019]: I understand the urgency here. Let's make sure we keep the client informed about our progress 😫 Fatima. We don't want them feeling left in the dark during this troubleshooting process.

Fatima [16:04 | 02/08/2019]: Definitely, Dave. 👍 I'll keep the client updated at regular intervals, providing them with any relevant information we uncover.

John [16:20 | 02/08/2019]: I've checked the codebase, and so far, I haven't found any obvious issues. It's strange that the app is crashing on load. Could it be a memory-related issue? Keith, do we have any recent reports of memory leaks or high memory usage?

Keith [16:22 | 02/08/2019]: I'll pull up the monitoring logs,
John, and check if there have been any memory-related anomalies
in recent releases. Let me get back to you on that.

Fatima [17:01 | 02/08/2019]: Quick update, everyone. The client
is using an iPhone X running iOS 15.1. They mentioned that the
issue started after updating their app a few days ago 😌

Keith [17:05 | 02/08/2019]: Thanks for the update, Fatima.
That's helpful information. John, let's focus on testing the
latest app update on an iPhone X simulator with iOS 15.1 to see
if we can replicate the issue.

John [17:06 | 02/08/2019]: Good idea, Keith. I'll set up the
emulator and run some tests right away.

Keith [17:30 | 02/08/2019]: John, any progress on replicating
the issue on the emulator?

John [17:32 | 02/08/2019]: Yes, Keith. I managed to reproduce
the crash on the emulator. It seems to be related to a
compatibility issue with iOS 15.1 🤯. I suspect it's due to a
deprecated method call. I'll fix it and run more tests to
confirm.

John [18:03 | 02/08/2019]: Fixed the deprecated method issue,
and the app is no longer crashing on load. It looks like we've
identified and resolved the problem. I'll prepare a patch and
send it to you, Keith, for review and deployment.

Keith [18:04 | 02/08/2019]: 👏👏👏 Thank you, please provide
me with the patch as soon as possible. Once I review it, we'll
deploy the fix to the app store.

Dave [18:06 | 02/08/2019]: Great job, team! 🎉 John, please keep the client informed about the progress and let them know we have a fix ready for them on the next app update. Can someone make sure the release notes reflect this?

John [18:07 | 02/08/2019]: Will do, Dave. I'll update the client and ensure they're aware of the upcoming fix.

Keith [18:27 | 02/08/2019]: Patch reviewed and approved, John. Please proceed with updating the app in the store. Let's aim to have it done within the next hour.

John [18:26 | 02/08/2019]: Understood, Keith. I'm in the process of uploading it now.

Fatima [18:38 | 02/08/2019]: I just informed the client about the fix. They're relieved and grateful for our prompt response. Thanks, everyone, for your collaboration and quick action. It's a pleasure working with such a competent team!

Dave [18:40 | 02/08/2019]: Well done, team! Your efforts are greatly appreciated. We managed to turn this urgent problem around in record time. Let's keep up the good work! 👍

Prompt Engineering 101: Text Summarization

So, needless to say, no one wants to spend their day constantly scrolling through Slack channels reading about issues and problems that are on fire. We're going to utilize the capabilities of ChatGPT for text summarization. To keep things simple, let's try a few prompts to send the entire listing of the chat messages to ChatGPT in order for it to give us a usable summary of all the events that have happened.

Prompt #1: "tl;dr"

This prompt is short, sweet, and to the point. In case you're not familiar
with it, it's a term used online frequently to briefly summarize a long
article. It literally stands for "Too Long; Didn't Read," which is how I feel
about a lot of conversations on Slack when I'm swamped with work.
Conveniently, ChatGPT can understand this simple term (I wouldn't
necessarily call it a word) as a prompt, and the results are pretty
impressive.

Listing 3-6. PROMPT. Asking for a Summarized Version of a Longer
Conversation

System: You are a helpful assistant
User: Fatima [16:00 | 02/08/2019]: Hey everyone, I have an
urgent ...
User: Tl;dr
Model: gpt-4
Temperature: 1
Maximum length: 360
Top P: 1
Frequency penalty: 0
Presence penalty: 0

Note   You have two options now on how to send the preceding
prompt to ChatGPT. The first option is to use the ChatGPTClient.
java app and its supporting classes. The second option is to use
the Chat Playground. In either case, be sure that the first User
message contains all of the text that is in Listing 3-5. It's truncated in
Listing 3-6 to make it more readable.

Notice how the number of tokens is kept small, at 360, which will ultimately help ChatGPT to create a short response. Also see that the temperature is left at 1 (the default value), but the Top P is increased all the way to its maximum (which is 1). Therefore, it's important to play around with temperature and other settings to control the tone and variety of ChatGPT's responses.

Listing 3-7 shows ChatGPT's summarization of the conversation from Listing 3-5.

Listing 3-7. RESPONSE. Getting a Summarized Version of a Very Long Conversation

```
The team quickly responds to a client's app crashing issue.
John investigates the codebase while Fatima gathers information
from the client. They discover a compatibility issue with iOS
15.1 and John fixes it. The patch is reviewed and approved,
and the app is updated in the store. The client is informed
and grateful for the quick resolution. The team is praised for
their collaboration and prompt action.
```

That's fantastic! It reduced that extremely long conversation down to a simple and brief summary of only 68 words. As you can see, ChatGPT is not replacing a job here; however, it will definitely make someone more productive. Now, let's try a few more prompts, shall we?

Prompt #2: "Explain This in 3 Sentences or Less"

So, If "tl;dr" doesn't provide a brief enough explanation for you, then we can tell ChatGPT to make things even simpler. ChatGPT does well with parameters, so let's specify that the explanation shouldn't be any longer than 3 sentences as shown in Listing 3-8.

Listing 3-8. PROMPT. Asking for a Shorter Version of a Longer Conversation

```
System: You are a helpful assistant
User:  Fatima [16:00 | 02/08/2019]: Hey everyone, I have an
urgent ...
User: Explain this in 3 sentences or less.
Model: gpt-4
Temperature: 1
Maximum length: 250
Top P: 0
Frequency penalty: 0
Presence penalty: 0
```

As you may have noticed, the temperature is set to 0.82 in this example. We really want ChatGPT to give us a concise answer here, so the "drier" the better.

Listing 3-9. RESPONSE. Getting a 3 Sentence Summary

```
A customer reported an urgent issue of app crashes to the
team. John investigates the issue and asks Fatima to gather
additional information from the client. They discover that the
```

issue is related to a compatibility problem with iOS 15.1. John
fixes the problem and Keith approves the deployment of the fix
to the client's production environment.

Prompt #3: "I'm a Manager. Explain to Me What Happened"

When you don't want to sound like the one person that doesn't
understand, ChatGPT has the capability to rephrase what has been said
and break it down until it's very simple (Listing 3-10).

Listing 3-10. PROMPT. Asking for a Simplified Version of a More
Complex Conversation

System: You are a helpful assistant
User: Fatima [16:00 | 02/08/2019]: Hey everyone, I have an
urgent ...
User: Summarize this conversation and explain it to me like I'm
a manager with little technical experience.
Model: gpt-3.5-turbo
Temperature: 0.82
Maximum length: 750
Top P: 1
Frequency penalty: 0
Presence penalty: 0

Again, the temperature is set below 1.0 so that ChatGPT can keep the
answer brief and easy to understand. We increased the token length so that
ChatGPT can take the time to explain some potentially technical concepts.

Listing 3-11. RESPONSE. Getting a Simplified Version of a More
Complex Conversation

In this conversation, Fatima brings up an urgent issue with a
client who is experiencing app crashes as soon as they load
it. Keith assigns John to investigate the issue since their
architect is out sick. John asks Fatima to gather additional
information from the client about their device, operating
system, and recent updates. Dave emphasizes the importance of
keeping the client informed throughout the troubleshooting
process.

John checks the codebase but doesn't find any obvious issues,
so he suspects it could be a memory-related problem. Keith
agrees to check for memory-related anomalies in recent
releases. Fatima provides an update that the client is using an
iPhone X running iOS 15.1 and mentioned that the issue started
after updating the app. Keith suggests testing the latest app
update on an iPhone X simulator with iOS 15.1 to replicate
the issue.

John successfully reproduces the crash on the emulator and
identifies a compatibility issue with iOS 15.1, possibly due
to a deprecated method call. He fixes the issue and prepares a
patch for review and deployment. Keith approves the patch and
asks John to update the app in the store. Dave requests that
the client be kept informed and that the release notes reflect
the upcoming fix.

John uploads the patch and informs the client about the fix.
Keith reviews and approves the patch, and John proceeds with
updating the app in the store. Fatima informs the client about
the fix, and they express relief and gratitude for the prompt
response. Dave commends the team for their collaboration
and quick action, emphasizing the importance of maintaining
good work.

In summary, the team quickly addressed an urgent issue where
a client's app was crashing on load. They investigated the
issue, identified a compatibility problem with iOS 15.1, fixed
it, and prepared a patch for deployment. The client was kept
informed throughout the process, and the fix was successfully
implemented, resulting in a relieved and grateful client.

Prompt #4: "Give Me Suggestions on Next Steps"

In addition to making a summary that's easier to understand, ChatGPT can
explain in different styles and "tones." We're going to increase the top P to
0.75 because we want ChatGPT to think of more possibilities than what
is the default. We are also going to increase the presence penalty to 0.5
because we want to encourage a versatile response.

Listing 3-12. PROMPT. Asking to ChatGPT for Advice on the Best
Next Steps

System: You are a helpful assistant
User: Fatima [16:00 | 02/08/2019]: Hey everyone, I have an
urgent ...
User: I'm a QA engineer at the company. Give me suggestions on
next steps.
Model: gpt-4

Temperature: 1
Maximum length: 1200
Top P: 0.75
Frequency penalty: 0
Presence penalty: 0.5

Listing 3-13. RESPONSE. Suggestions from ChatGPT on Possible Next Steps

As a QA engineer, here are some suggestions for next steps:

1. Test the patch: Once the patch has been deployed to the app store, thoroughly test it on various devices and operating systems to ensure that the issue has been resolved and there are no new bugs or regressions introduced.

2. Conduct regression testing: In addition to testing the specific issue, perform a comprehensive regression test to ensure that the fix does not have any unintended side effects on other functionalities of the app.

3. Communicate the fix to the client: Keep the client updated on the progress and let them know that the fix is available in the latest app update. Provide them with clear instructions on how to update their app and encourage them to test it on their end as well.

4. Monitor user feedback: Keep an eye on user feedback after the fix has been deployed. Encourage users to report any issues they encounter, and be proactive in addressing them promptly.

5. Document the issue and resolution: Create a detailed report documenting the issue, the steps taken to reproduce and resolve it, and any other relevant information. This will serve as a reference for future troubleshooting and help improve the development process.

6. Conduct a post-mortem analysis: After the issue has been resolved and the fix has been deployed, schedule a post-mortem meeting with the team to discuss the root cause, lessons learned, and any process improvements that can be implemented to prevent similar issues in the future.

7. Continuous improvement: Use this incident as an opportunity to identify areas of improvement in the development and testing processes. Evaluate if there are any changes that can be made to prevent similar issues from occurring in the future.

Remember, open communication, collaboration, and continuous learning are key to ensuring the highest quality of your app and maintaining a strong relationship with your clients.

Now, of course, ChatGPT (like every other form of artificial intelligence on the planet) is not entirely perfect. For instance, recommendation number 3 is a valid item to do, except for the fact that it's not usually the responsibility of a QA person in order to communicate anything directly to the client or customer. That communication can be done either through tech support, or with a product manager who has those communication channels (especially if they are a significant customer). So, the suggestion is fine, but it's not appropriate for a person with that role within a company.

Let's Talk About Real Prompt Engineering

If you Google the term, "prompt engineering," you'll find a ton of examples, blogs, and even full websites with subscription plans that will try to convince you that the perfect prompts can be created by simply only using text. As you have seen from the examples above, prompt engineering cannot be accomplished solely by merely crafting textual inputs.

In reality, the process is quite similar to cooking a sophisticated meal. Imagine trying to cook, for example, beef bourguignon using only salt as the seasoning, and neglecting all other ingredients and spices! Honestly, the result would pale in comparison to the actual dish.

Similarly, try assembling an entire orchestra but only use one instrument and one musician. That's an embarrassing "one man band." Therefore, simply adjusting the text to the prompt isn't enough in order to truly perform prompt engineering. The parameters such as the model's temperature, which controls randomness; the top-p, impacting token probability; the specific model used; the number of tokens; and the other parameters to the endpoint all play highly pivotal roles in getting a great response.

This book is not about prompt engineering, since (as you can see from the explanation above) it truly involves several factors that don't have anything to do with Java. However, you are highly encouraged to experiment with ALL the parameters to the models and endpoints provided by OpenAI to find what works best for your use case.

Registering a Slack Bot App

Now that we know the various ways for ChatGPT to summarize a large body of text for us, let's see what's necessary in order to create a simple bot in Java that will programmatically grab all the messages from a channel within a Slack instance.

Note   In order to accomplish the steps, you will need to have
administrative access to a Slack workspace. Most developers will
NOT have these levels of permissions; therefore, in order to fully
experiment, I recommend that you create your own personal Slack
workspace for testing purposes. This way, you will have all the rights
and privileges to install your Slack bot.

But one step at a time. First, we're going to make our Slack bot app, so
head over to Slack API website (Figure 3-1).

```
https://api.slack.com/
```

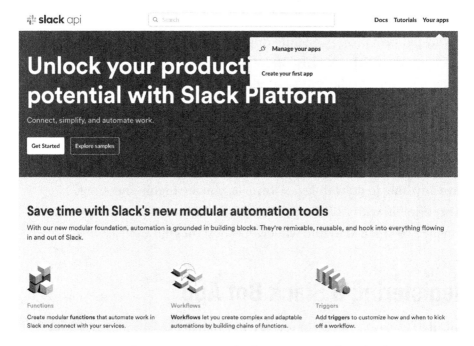

Figure 3-1. *In Order to Create a Slack Bot, Go to the Slack
API Website*

Of course, you'll need to have a Slack account in order for this to work, so if you don't have one, then you need to create one first.

After you have logged in, go to the top-right of the page and navigate to "**Your apps ➤ Create your first app**", as shown in Figure 3-1. In Slack terminology, a "bot" is an "app," and bots are not allowed to run on a Slack instance unless they have been registered with Slack first.

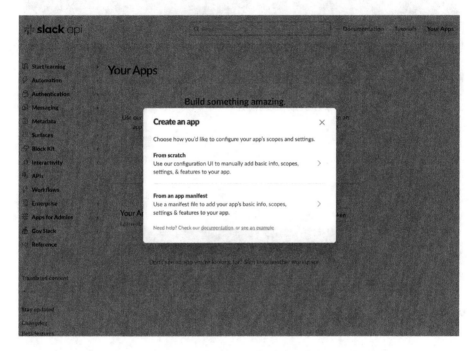

Figure 3-2. *Creating a New Bot App for Slack*

As shown in Figure 3-2, you'll be taken to the **Your Apps** page where you can manage your Slack apps. Immediately, you'll see a popup to **Create an App** button in the middle of the screen.

Select the option to create your app **from scratch**. This is because we want to be able to manipulate all of the details of the application ourselves without overcomplicating things with a bunch of default settings.

Afterward, you'll be prompted to specify a name for your bot and to select the workspace that you want your bot to have access to, as shown in Figure 3-3.

Click the **Create App** button to proceed.

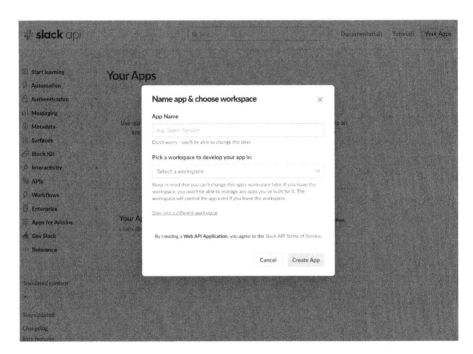

Figure 3-3. *Creating a New Bot App for Slack*

Specifying What Your Bot Can (and Can't) Do By Setting the Scope

Now, you'll be presented with a screen that has a ton of options for bots for Slack workspaces. The first thing you need to do, however, is from the sidebar on the left, click **OAuth & Permissions**.

Our bot is going to be pretty simple; all it needs to do is read the messages from a channel in order to give us a summary of what was said. In addition to reading the messages, we also need to know the

names of the people in the Slack workspace; otherwise, we'll get a
UUID representation of the person instead of their name, which is
meaningless to us.

So, scroll down and be sure to add the following OAuth Scopes to your
Slack Bot, as shown in Figure 3-4.

- channels:history

- channels:read

- users:read

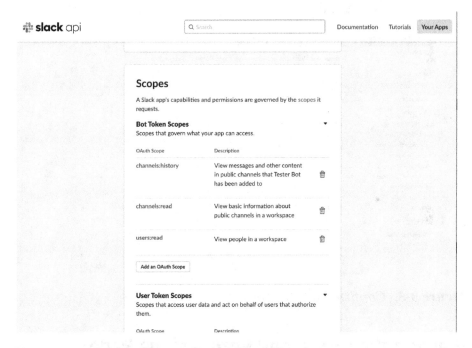

Figure 3-4. *Adding Scopes for the Slack Bot App*

Confirming Your Settings

After you've added the appropriate scopes for your bot, scroll back up and click **Basic Information** from the left side bar.

On the page that follows, you'll see that there's now a green checkmark beside "Add features and functionality," which confirms that you've added your scopes correctly, as shown in Figure 3-5.

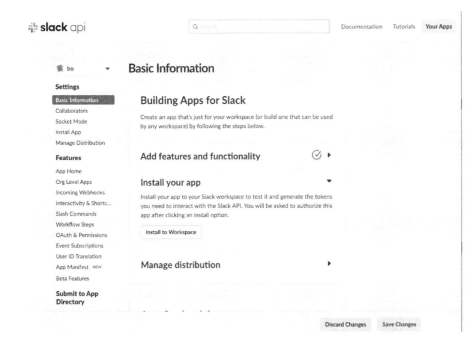

Figure 3-5. *Confirm Your Settings*

Viewing the OAuth and Permissions Page

As shown in Figure 3-6, navigate to the **OAuth & Permissions** page and click the "Install to Workspace" button.

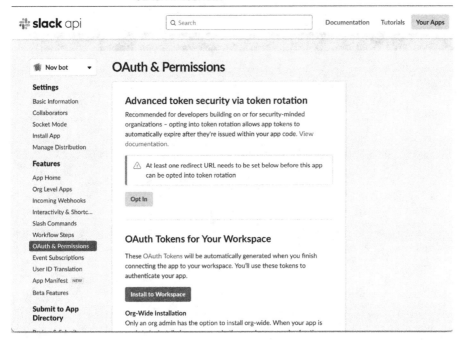

Figure 3-6. *The OAuth & Permission Screen*

Installing Your Slack Bot App to Your Workspace

Now that all the permissions have been requested, it's time to install your
bot to your workspace. During the installation process, you should see a
screen as shown in Figure 3-7.

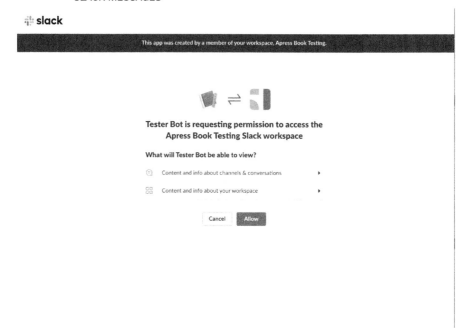

Figure 3-7. *"Installing" a New Slack Bot App*

Click the **Allow** button to authorize the bot and allow the permissions you allotted in the previous step.

Note   It's important to understand what "installing" means here. In a traditional Java sense, installing an app means to load a JAR, WAR, or EAR file into another machine and have it to execute. That's not what's happening here.

Here, when you "install" a bot app, you're enabling your Slack workspace to allow an app to join the workspace – that's all. The code for your bot will run on your own machine, and not on Slack's servers.

Getting Your Slack Bot (Access) Token

This time, "token," actually means access token! In order to connect to the
Slack API and access messages and user information programmatically,
you need a specific OAuth token generated for your Slack bot.

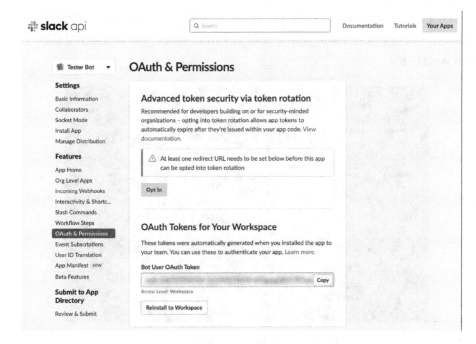

Figure 3-8. *Copy Your OAuth Token for Your Slack Bot App*

Back on the **OAuth & Permissions** page, be sure to copy the bot
token (which usually starts with "xoxb-") from the page here, as shown in
Figure 3-8.

Inviting Your Bot to Your Channel

Next, you're going to go to the channel you'd like to use to test your bot and type in the following command in the channel itself.

```
/invite
```

Select the option "**Add apps to this channel,**" and then select the name of the Slack Bot that you specified earlier when you registered the bot with Slack.

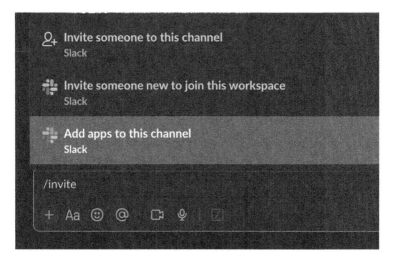

Figure 3-9. *Adding Your Slack Bot to a Channel*

Congratulations! You now have successfully registered a Slack Bot App with Slack, enabled it to read messages in your workspace, and added the Slack Bot to a channel. Before we can write the Java code to access the channel in our workspace, we need to know what is the internal ID that Slack uses for our channel.

Finding the Channel ID of Your Channel

Ok, this is an easy step to do. In Slack, right-click the name of your channel and select the option "**View Channel details.**" At the bottom of the popup window is the ID of your channel. Copy that number and save it for later. Your Java app will need this in order to join the right channel in your Slack workspace.

Using Your Slack Bot App to Automatically Grab Messages from a Channel

Alright, now that we have done all the prerequisites and we know the ID of our channel, let's get to the code in Java that accesses all the messages from a particular Slack channel.

Setting Up Your Dependencies

The Slack API library for Java provides convenient methods to interact with the Slack platform. Mostly everything that we need comes from the com. slack.api.methods.* or the com.slack.api.model.* packages, which exist in the slack-api-client-<VERSION> and the slack-api-model-<VERSION> jar files.

The Slack Java API has its own dependencies, which are

- GSON

  - gson-<VERSION>.jar

- Kotlin

  - kotlin-stdlib-<VERSION>.jar

  - kotlin-stdlib-jdk8-<VERSION>.jar

- OK HTTP and OK IO

  - okhttp-<VERSION>.jar

  - okio-<VERSION>.jar

  - okio-jvm-<VERSION>.jar

- SL4J

  - slf4j-api-<VERSION>.jar

Therefore, Listings 3-14 and 3-15 are snippets of the Maven pom.xml and Gradle build.gradle files necessary (with the versions that I tested with) in order to get everything to build.

Listing 3-14. Maven pom.xml

```
<dependencies>
    <!-- Gson library -->
    <dependency>
        <groupId>com.google.code.gson</groupId>
        <artifactId>gson</artifactId>
        <version>2.10.1</version>
    </dependency>

    <!-- Kotlin standard libraries -->
    <dependency>
        <groupId>org.jetbrains.kotlin</groupId>
        <artifactId>kotlin-stdlib</artifactId>
        <version>1.6.20</version>
    </dependency>
    <dependency>
        <groupId>org.jetbrains.kotlin</groupId>
        <artifactId>kotlin-stdlib-jdk8</artifactId>
        <version>1.6.20</version>
    </dependency>
```

```xml
<!-- OkHttp library -->
<dependency>
    <groupId>com.squareup.okhttp3</groupId>
    <artifactId>okhttp</artifactId>
    <version>4.11.0</version>
</dependency>

<!-- Okio library -->
<dependency>
    <groupId>com.squareup.okio</groupId>
    <artifactId>okio</artifactId>
    <version>3.2.0</version>
</dependency>
<dependency>
    <groupId>com.squareup.okio</groupId>
    <artifactId>okio-jvm</artifactId>
    <version>3.2.0</version>
</dependency>

<!-- Slack SDK libraries -->
<dependency>
    <groupId>com.slack.api</groupId>
    <artifactId>slack-api-client</artifactId>
    <version>1.30.0</version>
</dependency>
<dependency>
    <groupId>com.slack.api</groupId>
    <artifactId>slack-api-model</artifactId>
    <version>1.30.0</version>
</dependency>

<!-- SLF4J logging facade -->
<dependency>
```

```
            <groupId>org.slf4j</groupId>
            <artifactId>slf4j-api</artifactId>
            <version>2.0.7</version>
        </dependency>
    </dependencies>
```

Listing 3-15. Gradle build.gradle

```
dependencies {
    // Gson library
    implementation 'com.google.code.gson:gson:2.10.1'

    // Kotlin standard libraries
    implementation 'org.jetbrains.kotlin:kotlin-stdlib:1.6.20'
    implementation 'org.jetbrains.kotlin:kotlin-stdlib-
    jdk8:1.6.20'

    // OkHttp library
    implementation 'com.squareup.okhttp3:okhttp:4.11.0'

    // Okio library
    implementation 'com.squareup.okio:okio:3.2.0'
    implementation 'com.squareup.okio:okio-jvm:3.2.0'

    // Slack SDK libraries
    implementation 'com.slack.api:slack-api-client:1.30.0'
    implementation 'com.slack.api:slack-api-model:1.30.0'

    // SLF4J logging facade
    implementation 'org.slf4j:slf4j-api:2.0.7'
}

compileKotlin {
    kotlinOptions {
        jvmTarget = "1.8"
```

```
        }
    }
    compileTestKotlin {
        kotlinOptions {
            jvmTarget = "1.8"
        }
    }
}
```

Now that we have our access token, as well as all of our necessary
dependencies, let's look at the code necessary in order to access a channel
and grab all the chat history within a specified time range. For obvious
purposes, we want the user name, timestamp, and message content of
each posting in the channel.

Programmatically Reading Messages from Slack with ChannelReaderSlackBot.java

Listing 3-16 is a simple Java Slack Bot that obtains the user name,
timestamp, and message content of each posting in the channel within a
designated time period.

Listing 3-16. ChannelReaderSlackBot.java

```
import com.slack.api.Slack;
import com.slack.api.methods.MethodsClient;
import com.slack.api.methods.request.conversations.
ConversationsHistoryRequest;
import com.slack.api.methods.response.conversations.
ConversationsHistoryResponse;
import com.slack.api.methods.request.users.UsersInfoRequest;
import com.slack.api.methods.response.users.UsersInfoResponse;
import com.slack.api.model.Message;
```

```java
import com.slack.api.model.User;
import com.slack.api.model.block.LayoutBlock;

import java.time.*;
import java.util.Collections;
import java.util.List;

public class ChannelReaderSlackBot {

        private static final String SLACK_BOT_TOKEN = "YOUR_
        SLACK_API_TOKEN";

        public static void main(String[] args) {
        Slack slack = Slack.getInstance();
        MethodsClient methods = slack.methods(SLACK_BOT_TOKEN);

        String channelId = "YOUR_CHANNEL_ID";

        LocalDateTime startTimeUTC = LocalDateTime.of(2023,
        Month.AUGUST, 3, 10, 0);
        LocalDateTime endTimeUTC = LocalDateTime.of(2023,
        Month.AUGUST, 12, 15, 0);

        long startTime = startTimeUTC.atZone(ZoneOffset.UTC).
        toEpochSecond();
        long endTime = endTimeUTC.atZone(ZoneOffset.UTC).
        toEpochSecond();

        ConversationsHistoryRequest request =
        ConversationsHistoryRequest.builder()
            .channel(channelId)
            .oldest(String.valueOf(startTime))
            .latest(String.valueOf(endTime))
            .build();
```

```java
try {
    ConversationsHistoryResponse response = methods.
    conversationsHistory(request);

    if (response != null && response.isOk()) {
        List<Message> messages = response.
        getMessages();
        Collections.reverse(messages);
        for (Message message : messages) {
            String userId = message.getUser();
            String timestamp = formatTimestamp(message.
            getTs());

            UsersInfoRequest userInfoRequest =
            UsersInfoRequest.builder()
                .user(userId)
                .build();

            UsersInfoResponse userInfoResponse =
            methods.usersInfo(userInfoRequest);
            if (userInfoResponse != null &&
            userInfoResponse.isOk()) {
                User user = userInfoResponse.getUser();
                System.out.println("User: " + user.
                getName());
                System.out.println("Timestamp: " +
                timestamp);
                System.out.println("Message: " +
                message.getText());
                System.out.println();
            }
        }
    } else {
```

```
            System.out.println("Failed to fetch messages: "
            + response.getError());
        }
    } catch (Exception e) {
        e.printStackTrace();
    }
}

private static String formatTimestamp(String ts) {
    double timestamp = Double.parseDouble(ts);
    Instant instant = Instant.ofEpochSecond((long)
    timestamp);
    LocalDateTime dateTime = LocalDateTime.
    ofInstant(instant, ZoneOffset.UTC);
    return dateTime.toString();
}
}
```

Of course, you should replace "YOUR_SLACK_API_TOKEN" with your actual Slack API token and "YOUR_CHANNEL_ID" with the ID of the Slack channel you want to read the messages from.

If you want to do something very basic, the Slack Java API is actually quite simple to use. You can't do anything without first getting an instance of the "Slack" class itself using the static call "Slack.getInstance()" method. This connects to the underlying Slack API infrastructure allowing you to interact with the exposed methods and retrieve the information that we want.

Next, we need an instance of the "MethodsClient" class by invoking the "slack.methods()" method, where we provide our access token.

In order to retrieve the chat history, we use the
ConversationsHistoryRequest class which is another class provided by the
Slack API. Here, all you need to do is specify the desired channel ID, the
oldest timestamp, and the latest timestamp to define the time range for the
chat history. In this example, we retrieve messages from August 3, 2023, at
10:00 to August 12, 2023, at 15:00. Easy peasy.

Listing 3-17 shows the output after executing ChannelReaderSlackBot.
java, which is truncated here since you already have the full text in
Listing 3-5 earlier in this chapter.

Listing 3-17. The Output from Executing
ChannelReaderSlackBot.java

```
Fatima [2023-08-11T09:04:20] : Hey everyone, I have an urgent
issue to discuss. I just got off a call with a client who's
experiencing app crashes as soon as they load it. They're
really frustrated. Can we get this sorted ASAP? :tired_face:

Keith [2023-08-11T09:04:35] : Thanks for bringing this to our
attention, Fatima. Let's jump on this right away. John, can you
take the lead in investigating the issue since our architect is
out sick today?

John [2023-08-11T09:04:52] : Sure thing, Keith. I'll dive into
the codebase and see if I can find any potential culprits for
the crashes.

John [2023-08-11T09:05:30] : Fatima, could you gather some
additional information from the client? Ask them about the
specific device, operating system, and any recent updates they
might have installed.

...
```

Exercises Left for the Reader

So, there are obviously a few additional things we can do here, and these steps will be left for you (the reader) to accomplish, for example:

- Making the `ChatGPTClient.java` (the related classes) to be even more safe for novice users. For example, for ChatGPT, the valid value for the top P parameter is only between 0 and 1. The constructor for the Chat.java class should throw an Exception if the user specifies anything that is beyond the range of any valid values.

- Connecting the code in `ChannelReaderSlackBot.java` that reads the messages from Slack to the `ChatGPTClient.java` so that grabbing the messages and getting a summary is a single step process.

- Adding more capabilities to the Slack bot itself such as adding commands so that anyone in the channel can request a summary. In its current state, the bot doesn't post anything in the channel. However, the "user interface" to the bot is the channel itself; therefore, someone should be able to interact with the Slack bot by typing a command (such as requesting a summary).

- Making sure that the bot doesn't make a bad situation worse. Whenever the bot provides a summary, it should not post in the channel itself because that could add a lot of noise to an already noisy situation. The best practice is to have the bot send a private message to the person asking for a summary (or whatever new command that you create).

Conclusion

In this chapter, we talked about one of the various ways artificial intelligence can be put to practical use within the enterprise today. We showed you how to improve upon our `ChatGPTClient.java` application by utilizing the builder pattern in order to allow constructing your class to be a lot more flexible than what was in the previous chapter.

Most notably, however, we discussed what is truly "prompt engineering," by discussing that prompt engineering cannot be accomplished by simply textual input to ChatGPT alone. You definitely need to understand the ramifications of all the input parameters to the ChatGPT API, in order to properly, and effectively, perform prompt engineering.

Using what we learned about prompt engineering, we were able to successfully obtain summarizations of any large body of text provided to us. Finally, we saw the code necessary in order to run an automated bot that will grab messages from any Slack channel programmatically, if we specify a valid date range.

In this chapter (as well as the previous chapter), we were working exclusively with the Chat Completions Endpoint of the OpenAI APIs. In the next chapter, we're going to push the boundaries of what's possible by experimenting with the Whisper and DALL·E Endpoints.

CHAPTER 4

Multimodal AI: Creating a Podcast Visualizer with Whisper and DALL·E 3

Now let's introduce a new term: **multimodal AI**. In the most simplest of terms, generative AI models can create content in 1 of 4 formats:

- Text
- Audio
- Images
- Video

Each of those formats is a **mode**. Multimodal AI is the process of using multiple AI models together to generate (or to understand) content where the input is one type of mode and the output is a different type of mode.

© Bruce Hopkins 2024
B. Hopkins, *ChatGPT for Java*, https://doi.org/10.1007/979-8-8688-0116-7_4

Take, for example, OpenAI's Whisper model. If you provide it audio, it is able to create a transcription of everything said into text. The same thing applies to DALL·E. If you supply it with a textual prompt, then it is able to generate an image of what you described.

In this chapter, we're going to take multimodal AI to the next level! As an avid podcast listener, I've often wondered what the scenery, the imagery, the characters, the subject, or the background looked like while listening to a very immersive story in audio format.

So we're going to create a Podcast Visualizer using multiple models from OpenAI. There are a few steps involved, but the final results are stunning. While listening to a podcast about a guy cooking some amazing things with tofu (don't knock it until you try it), the Podcast Visualizer came up with the image in Figure 4-1.

Figure 4-1. *The AI-Generated Result of Visualizing a Podcast About Tofu Using the GPT-4, Whisper, and DALL·E Models*

In order to make the code for the Podcast Visualizer easy to follow along, we'll do things separately in the following three steps:

- Step-1: Take a podcast episode and use the Whisper model to get a transcript.

- Step-2: Take the resulting transcript and use the GTP-4 model to describe the visual aspects of what's being discussed in the podcast episode.

- Step-3: Take the resulting description and use the DALL·E model to generate an image.

The code presented here in this chapter has tons of practical uses, for example:

- If you're just curious about the things in a podcast episode could look like (which is always the case for me), you can get a simple representative visual image to associate with what you're listening to.

- For people who are hearing impaired, you can easily turn a podcast or radio program into a slide-show of images. This greatly enhances the accessibility of the content.

- For podcasters, you can now have a simple way to add a visual/hero image to each of your episodes. This is useful since podcast players such as Apple Podcasts and Spotify allow podcasters to display a single image to associate with an individual episode. This can help with engagement for your listeners.

Introducing the Whisper Model by OpenAI

Now let's introduce another new term: **Automatic Speech Recognition** (ASR). The average everyday consumer is very familiar with this technology due to its integration into mobile phones (e.g., Siri for the iPhone) and smart speakers (e.g., any Alexa device). At its core, ASR technology converts spoken language into text.

Whisper is OpenAI's model for speech recognition, and the accuracy is astonishingly high. Listing 4-1 is a transcript of an episode of the very popular DuoLingo Spanish podcast, which makes the Spanish language easy to be understood by English listeners by combining both English and Spanish together in a woven narrative story. The transcript was generated using the Whisper model.

Listing 4-1. The Whisper Model Performs Speech Recognition to Convert Audio Into Text

```
...I'm Martina Castro. Every episode we bring you fascinating,
true stories to help you improve your Spanish listening and
gain new perspectives on the world. The storyteller will be
using intermediate Spanish and I'll be chiming in for context
in English. If you miss something, you can always skip back
and listen again. We also offer full transcripts at podcast.
duolingo.com.

Growing up, Linda was fascinated with her grandmother, Erlinda.
Erlinda was a healer or curandera, someone who administers
remedies for mental, emotional, physical, or spiritual
illnesses.

In Guatemala, this is a practice passed down orally through
generations in the same family. Mal de ojo, or the evil eye, is
considered an illness by many Guatemalans who believe humans
have the power to transfer bad energy to others. Neighbors
```

```
would bring their babies to Linda's grandmother when they
suspected an energy imbalance. Su madre lo llevaba a nuestra
casa para curarlo...
```

If you've ever worked with a speech recognition system before (even with sophisticated technologies like Siri and Alexa), you will know that it has problems, for instance:

- **Speech recognition has problems with punctuation**

    - Have you noticed that nobody speaks with punctuation? For the English language, we use changes in tone or volume to ask a question or give an exclamation. We also use short and long pauses for commas and periods.

- **Speech recognition has problems with foreign words and accents**

    - Depending on who you ask, there are at least 170k words in the English language. However, in conversational English, we are always using foreign words like

        - Tsunami (Japanese origin): A large sea wave often caused by an earthquake

        - Hors d'oeuvre (French origin): An appetizer

        - Lingerie (French origin): Women's underwear or nightclothes

        - Aficionado (Spanish origin): Someone who is very passionate about a specific activity or subject

        - Piñata (Spanish origin): A brightly colored box of candy for kids to beat relentlessly

- **Speech recognition has problems with names**

  - Certain names of people, businesses, and websites can often be hard to spell and understand

- **Speech recognition has problems with homophones**

  - Do you remember those words that **sound the same** but have different spellings and meanings? The fantastic editor of this book knows all of them!

    - Would / Wood

    - Flour / Flower

    - Two / Too / To

    - They're / There / Their

    - Pair / Pare / Pear

    - Break / Brake

    - Allowed / Aloud

As you can see from Listing 4-1, Whisper was able to understand all the punctuation in the audio, identify all the foreign words (of which there were several), and understand the names as well as the company name ("duolingo") within a URL! Of course, if you noticed, it could also understand the difference between "wood" and "would."

Features and Limitations of the Whisper Model

The Whisper model is able to convert spoken audio from the following languages into text:

- Afrikaans
- Arabic
- Armenian
- Azerbaijani
- Belarusian
- Bosnian
- Bulgarian
- Catalan
- Chinese
- Croatian
- Czech
- Danish
- Dutch
- **English** (of course!)
- Estonian
- Finnish
- French
- Galician
- German

- Greek

- Hebrew

- Hindi

- Hungarian

- Icelandic

- Indonesian

- Italian

- Japanese

- Kannada

- Kazakh

- Korean

- Latvian

- Lithuanian

- Macedonian

- Malay

- Marathi

- Maori

- Nepali

- Norwegian

- Persian

- Polish

- Portuguese

- Romanian

- Russian

- Serbian

- Slovak

- Slovenian

- Spanish

- Swahili

- Swedish

- Tagalog

- Tamil

- Thai

- Turkish

- Ukrainian

- Urdu

- Vietnamese

- Welsh

So, at the end of the day, it will be able to understand audio spoken by yourself and probably any language spoken by your friends and colleagues.

Developers are limited to send no more than 50 requests per minute to the endpoint, so this constraint needs to be taken into consideration if you want to transcribe vast amounts of audio.

Whisper supports audio in flac, mp3, mp4, mpeg, mpga, m4a, ogg, wav, or webm formats. Regardless of the format that you use, the maximum file size to send to the endpoint is 25MB.

Now, if you haven't worked extensively with audio files, please be aware that some formats create REALLY HUGE files (e.g., wav format), and others create really small files (e.g., m4a format). So, converting your file to a different format can help you with the 25MB limitation. However, later in this chapter, we'll see the code for a tool that takes a single large audio file and splits it into multiple, smaller files.

Transcriptions Endpoint

The Transcriptions Endpoint is a REST service that converts audio into text, and is only compatible with the Whisper model.

Creating the Request

Table 4-1 lists all the HTTP parameters necessary to call the Transcriptions Endpoint.

Table 4-1. *The HTTP Parameters for the Transcriptions Endpoint*

HTTP Param	Description
Endpoint URL	https://api.openai.com/v1/audio/transcriptions
Method	POST
Header	Authorization: Bearer **$OPENAI_API_KEY**
Content-Type	multipart/form-data

Note   Pay close attention to the content-type in the preceding table! Unlike the Chat Endpoint that sends all HTTP request parameters as a JSON object, the Transcriptions Endpoint only accepts parameters as **Form data elements**. If you try to send a well-formatted (or even a poorly formatted) JSON object, the Transcriptions Endpoint will return a very opaque error.

Request Body (Multipart Form Data)

Table 4-2. *The Request Body for Whisper*

Field	Type	Required?	Description
File	file	Required	The entire audio file that you want to be transcribed.
			Accepted formats are • flac • mp3 • mp4 • mpeg • mpga • m4a • ogg • wav • webm
Model	String	Required	The ID of the model that you want to use for transcription.
			Compatible models include • whisper-1

(*continued*)

Table 4-2. (*continued*)

Field	Type	Required?	Description
prompt	String	Optional	This is any text that can be provided to change the model's transcription style or to provide it with more context from a previous segment of audio.
			Be sure that the prompt is in the same language as the audio for best results.
			Additionally, this field can be used to change the spelling or capitalization of any words that Whisper is not familiar with.
response_format	String default: json	Optional	This is the format of the output of transcription.
			Accepted formats are • json • text • srt • verbose_json • vtt

(*continued*)

Table 4-2. (*continued*)

Field	Type	Required?	Description
temperature	Number default: 0	Optional	This is the sampling temperature, ranging from 0 to 1. A higher value increases the randomness of the output, whereas a lower value ensures a more deterministic output.
language	String	Optional	This is the language of the input audio. It's optional, but providing the value can improve the accuracy and latency for the transcription.

Creating a Utility App to Split Audio Files: `AudioSplitter.java`

So, we're almost at the point where we are able to programmatically invoke the Whisper model using the Transcriptions Endpoint. However, the Whisper Model has a limitation of 25MB per file.

Now, this is not a problem if you're listening to, for example, the StarDate podcast from the University of Texas at Austin. This podcast gives you a great glimpse of what to look for in the nighttime sky in about 2 minutes of audio.

However, that's not the case for other audio programs which tend to last for up to an hour (or even more). In cases like that, you're going to definitely exceed the 25MB file limitation.

Therefore, let's pair-program with ChatGPT and use our human intelligence to create our own utility that will take a single audio file and split it into multiple smaller files.

Note   In this section, I'm presenting one of many possibilities available on how to segment a large audio file into smaller pieces. For instance, you can use popular audio editing apps (such as the Open Source tool, Audacity, or the licensed tool, Adobe Audition) to manually cut up a large file into smaller files.

Listing 4-2 is the prompt that I sent to ChatGPT in order to get a basic app that splits audio files.

Listing 4-2. PROMPT. Using ChatGPT to Create the AudioSplitter. java App

System: You are a Java developer
User: Write an application that takes as input a single MP3 file and splits the file into contiguous segments no longer than 10 minutes. Name the file, "AudioSplitter.java"

After a little back and forth, I was able to create (as shown in Listing 4-3) the AudioSplitter.Java application that includes my edits to what was generated by ChatGPT.

Listing 4-3. RESPONSE. AudioSplitter.java

```
import org.bytedeco.javacv.FFmpegFrameGrabber;
import org.bytedeco.javacv.FFmpegFrameRecorder;

import java.io.IOException;

public class AudioSplitter {
        public static void main(String[] args) {
        String inputFilePath = "path/to/file/sample.mp3";
        String outputDirectory = "path/to/folder/";
        int segmentDurationInSeconds = 600; // 10 minutes
        in seconds

        try (FFmpegFrameGrabber grabber = new FFmpegFrameGrabber
        (inputFilePath)) {
            grabber.start();

            long totalDurationInSeconds = (long) grabber.
            getLengthInTime() / 1000000; // Convert
            microseconds to seconds
            double frameRate = grabber.getFrameRate();

            long segmentStartTime = 0;
            long segmentEndTime;
            int segmentNumber = 1;

            while (segmentStartTime < totalDurationInSeconds) {
                String outputFilePath = outputDirectory +
                "segment_" + segmentNumber + ".mp3";
```

```
try (FFmpegFrameRecorder recorder = new FFmpeg
FrameRecorder(outputFilePath, 0)) {
    recorder.setAudioChannels(2);
    recorder.setAudioCodecName("libmp3lame");
    // Set the audio codec to MP3
    recorder.setAudioBitrate(192000); // Adjust
    bitrate as needed
    recorder.setSampleRate(44100); // Adjust
    sample rate as needed
    recorder.setFrameRate(frameRate);
    recorder.setFormat("mp3"); // Set the
    output format to MP3
    recorder.start();

    segmentEndTime = Math.min(segmentStartTime
    + segmentDurationInSeconds,
    totalDurationInSeconds);

    grabber.setTimestamp(segmentStartTime *
    1000000); // Set the grabber's timestamp to
    the start time in microseconds

    while (grabber.getTimestamp() / 1000000 <
    segmentEndTime) {
        recorder.record(grabber.grabSamples());
    }
}

segmentStartTime = segmentEndTime;
segmentNumber++;
    }
} catch (IOException e) {
```

```
        e.printStackTrace();
    }
  }
}
```

Since the standard Java libraries don't have wide support for various media formats, we're using a combination of the FFmpeg library and JavaCV (both are free and open source).

The goal is simple: split an MP3 file into contiguous segments no longer than 10 minutes using the Java language. In this simple app, we do the following steps:

- First of all, we specify the input file path, output directory, and the desired segment duration in seconds (10 minutes).

- Next, we use the FFmpegFrameGrabber to open the input MP3 file and gather information about it, such as frame rate, audio codec, sample rate, and more.

- Afterward, we iterate through the input MP3 file, segmenting it into smaller parts of the specified duration (10 minutes or less). For each segment, we create a new FFmpegFrameRecorder, set its parameters, and record the frames within the segment duration.

- Finally, we increment the segment start time and segment number for each segment until we've processed the entire input MP3 file.

In order for this to work, you need to have the JavaCV and FFmpeg libraries properly installed and configured in your project.

Note   FFmpeg is an open source binary that you will need to install on your machine and be placed in your PATH or made accessible within your project. JavaCV uses FFmpeg via JNI (the Java Native Interface).

FFmpeg is an extremely versatile media converter which not only handles MP3 audio files, but various other audio file formats (including M4A, OGG, and WAV). It is able to convert video formats as well as static images like PNG, JPEG, and GIF.

After running the AudioSplitter.java utility on an MP3 file, you'll have a folder full of segmented audio files that are ten minutes long or less. Using the AudioSplitter.java utility, you have everything within a single Java file to modify the settings that work best for you. For our purposes, the goal here is to have audio files that are <25MB, so if you're transcribing 8-hr legal proceedings, for example, in WAV format, you may need to adjust the duration to be shorter, like 6 mins in length.

When using the AudioSplitter, the best practice is to have the output folder to be a different folder from the input, and you'll see why when we start to invoke the Transcriptions Endpoint using the Whisper model.

Creating the Audio Transcriber: `WhisperClient.java`

Now, let's build our next Java app, WhisperClient.java. Again, we're going to pair-program with ChatGPT to get a basis to work with. This time, we're going to ask for the OK HTTP library to be used for this app for two reasons:

- We've already used the library in Chapter 3 for the Slack Bot app.

- The OK HTTP library makes things a bit easier to use when working with HTTP multipart forms.

Listing 4-4 is the prompt to put in the Chat Playground to get things started. Be sure to note that I'm asking for a 60-sec HTTP request timeout since Whisper may take a little while to generate the transcript.

Listing 4-4. PROMPT: Asking ChatGPT to Convert cURL to Java and Send to Whisper's API

System: You are a Java developer.

User: Convert the following code from cURL to Java, using OkHttp to send the request. Make sure that I have a 60 second timeout on my request. Iterate over a single folder on my local computer and send all the files in the folder to the webservice. Name the file, WhisperClient.java.

User: curl https://api.openai.com/v1/audio/transcriptions \
  -H "Authorization: Bearer $OPENAI_API_KEY" \
  -H "Content-Type: multipart/form-data" \
  -F file="@/path/to/file/audio.mp3" \
  -F model="whisper-1"

Model: gpt-4

Temperature: 1

Maximum Length: 1150

After some back and forth, here's the response ChatGPT gave us that worked, as shown in Listing 4-5.

Listing 4-5. RESPONSE: WhisperClient.java

```
import java.io.*;
import java.nio.file.*;
import okhttp3.*;
import java.util.*;
import java.util.concurrent.TimeUnit;
import java.util.stream.Collectors;
import java.util.stream.Stream;

/**
 * Client class to transcribe MP3 files using the OpenAI
   Whisper model.
 */
public class WhisperClient {

    public static void main(String[] args) throws IOException {
        // API key for OpenAI (this should be replaced with
           your actual API key)
        String openAIKey = "";
        // OpenAI transcription endpoint
        String endpoint = "https://api.openai.com/v1/audio/
        transcriptions";
        // Model used for transcription
        String model = "whisper-1";
        // Media type for the MP3 files
        MediaType MEDIA_TYPE_MP3 = MediaType.
        parse("audio/mpeg");
```

```java
// Folder containing the MP3 files to be transcribed
String mp3FolderPath = "/Users/me/audio/segments";
// Desired format for the transcription response
String responseFormat = "text";

// Configure the HTTP client with specified timeouts
OkHttpClient client = new OkHttpClient.Builder()
    .connectTimeout(60, TimeUnit.SECONDS)
    .writeTimeout(60, TimeUnit.SECONDS)
    .readTimeout(60, TimeUnit.SECONDS)
    .build();

// List to store all mp3 files from the directory
List<File> mp3Files = new ArrayList<>();

// Try to collect all mp3 files in the directory and
//   store them in the list
try (Stream<Path> paths = Files.walk(Paths.
get(mp3FolderPath))) {
    mp3Files = paths
        .filter(Files::isRegularFile)
        .filter(p -> p.toString().endsWith(".mp3"))
        .map(Path::toFile)
        .sorted(Comparator.comparing(File::getName)) //
        Sort the files alphabetically
        .collect(Collectors.toList());
} catch (IOException e) {
    System.out.println("File reading error: " +
    e.getMessage());
    return; // Exit if there's an error reading
    the files
}
```

```java
// Iterate over each MP3 file, transcribe it, and print
   the response
for (File mp3File : mp3Files) {
    // Construct the request body for transcription
    RequestBody requestBody = new MultipartBody.
    Builder()
        .setType(MultipartBody.FORM)
        .addFormDataPart(
            "file",
            mp3File.getName(),
            RequestBody.create(mp3File, MEDIA_
            TYPE_MP3))
        .addFormDataPart("model", model)
        .addFormDataPart("response_format",
        responseFormat)
        .build();

    // Build the HTTP request
    Request request = new Request.Builder()
        .url(endpoint)
        .header("Authorization", "Bearer " + openAIKey)
        .post(requestBody)
        .build();

    // Make the request and process the response
    try (Response response = client.newCall(request).
    execute()) {
        if (!response.isSuccessful()) throw new
        IOException("Unexpected code " + response);
        System.out.println(response.body().string());
    } catch (IOException e) {
```

```
            System.out.println("Request error for file: " +
            mp3File.getName() + " - " + e.getMessage());
        }
    }
  }
}
```

As you can see, the `OkHttpClient` class allows us to use the Builder pattern to create an instance of the class with the timeouts we specified.

Now, here's the reason why it's a good idea when using the AudioSplitter.java utility to make the output folder separate from the input folder. We're creating a Collection of all the MP3 files from within a directory. More specifically, it's a "List<File>" that's named "mp3Files" to hold all the files that we want transcribed. Therefore, if the file that we want to be split into smaller segments is in the same folder with the segments themselves, then we'll be sending the large file (the one that's >25MB file) along with the smaller files to the Transcription Endpoint, which defeats the whole purpose of using the AudioSplitter.java app.

Therefore, the "Files.walk()" method allows us to recursively traverse the "mp3FolderPath" directory and collect all MP3 files and filter out those that do not end with the ".mp3" extension (for safety purposes, and to prevent any errors with the web service). Then, we map each "Path" to its corresponding "File" object and sort the files alphabetically based on their names. Finally, we use the "Collectors.toList()" method to collect all the sorted files into the "mp3Files" list.

With a Collection of MP3 files in hand, it's now time to send them to the Transcription Endpoint. As we build the RequestBody, the most important lines you should pay attention to are

```
.addFormDataPart("model", model)
.addFormDataPart("response_format", responseFormat)
```

That's due to the fact that if you want to add any optional parameters to the HTTP Request, (refer to Table 4-2 for all the parameters) such as the prompt or temperature, then you need to add them here in the same way that we specified the model and the response format.

Note   Let me reiterate – invoking the Transcriptions Endpoint is completely different from the Chat Endpoint. You may have already noticed one of the major differences between ChatGPTClient.java and WhisperClient.java are the import statements. ChatGPTClient. java (in Chapters 2 and 3) have the Jackson library within its import statements since we need to send the request as a JSON object. However, the imports in WhisperClient.java have no mention of Jackson, since we're sending everything as form data.

Having a Little Fun and Trying Things Out with a Podcast

Ok, so let's run a test using the code that we have presented so far. "This American Life" is a weekly public radio program (and also a podcast) that's hosted by Ira Glass and produced in collaboration with WBEZ Chicago.

Figure 4-2. *If You're Looking for a Good Podcast With Compelling Stories, I Recommend Listening to "This American Life"*
Image credit: WBEZ Chicago

Each episode weaves together a series of stories centered around a specific theme or topic. Some stories are investigative journalism, and others are simply interviews with ordinary people with captivating stories. Episode 811 is entitled "The one place I can't go," and the file is 56MB in MP3 format. Since we already know that 56MB is way too big to send to Whisper to get transcribed, Listing 4-6 shows the output from AudioSplitter.java on the MP3 file.

Listing 4-6. The Result of Running AudioSplitter.java on Episode 811 of This American Life

```
[mp3 @ 0x139e9c6a0] Estimating duration from bitrate, this may
be inaccurate
Input #0, mp3, from '/Users/me/thislife/ep811.mp3':
  Metadata:
    encoder         : Lavf58.78.100
    comment         : preroll_1;postroll_1
```

```
 Duration: 00:58:58.34, start: 0.000000, bitrate: 128 kb/s
  Stream #0:0: Audio: mp3, 44100 Hz, stereo, fltp, 128 kb/s
Output #0, mp3, to '/Users/me/thislife/segments/segment_1.mp3':
  Metadata:
    TSSE            : Lavf60.3.100
  Stream #0:0: Audio: mp3, 44100 Hz, stereo, fltp, 192 kb/s
[libmp3lame @ 0x139ea92e0] 2 frames left in the queue
on closing
Output #0, mp3, to '/Users/me/thislife/segments/segment_2.mp3':
  Metadata:
    TSSE            : Lavf60.3.100
  Stream #0:0: Audio: mp3, 44100 Hz, stereo, fltp, 192 kb/s
[libmp3lame @ 0x13b167720] 2 frames left in the queue
on closing
Output #0, mp3, to '/Users/me/thislife/segments/segment_3.mp3':
  Metadata:
    TSSE            : Lavf60.3.100
  Stream #0:0: Audio: mp3, 44100 Hz, stereo, fltp, 192 kb/s
[libmp3lame @ 0x13b166df0] 2 frames left in the queue
on closing
Output #0, mp3, to '/Users/me/thislife/segments/segment_4.mp3':
  Metadata:
    TSSE            : Lavf60.3.100
  Stream #0:0: Audio: mp3, 44100 Hz, stereo, fltp, 192 kb/s
[libmp3lame @ 0x13b166df0] 2 frames left in the queue
on closing
Output #0, mp3, to '/Users/me/thislife/segments/segment_5.mp3':
  Metadata:
    TSSE            : Lavf60.3.100
  Stream #0:0: Audio: mp3, 44100 Hz, stereo, fltp, 192 kb/s
[libmp3lame @ 0x139ea35f0] 2 frames left in the queue
on closing
```

```
Output #0, mp3, to '/Users/me/thislife/segments/segment_6.mp3':
  Metadata:
    TSSE            : Lavf60.3.100
  Stream #0:0: Audio: mp3, 44100 Hz, stereo, fltp, 192 kb/s
[libmp3lame @ 0x139ea3540] 2 frames left in the queue
on closing
```

Since the AudioSplitter.java utility uses a JNI wrapper to interface with FFmpeg, you'll see a lot of diagnostic messages during the audio splitting process, as shown in Listing 4-6. Unless you care about codecs, frequencies, and bitrates, most of the information presented will be meaningless to you. The good news, however, is that we now have a folder with 6 MP3 files ready for transcription!

Of course, as you can see from the code in Listing 4-5, WhisperClient. java iterates over all the files in a folder and send them to the Transcription Endpoint in order to use the Whisper Model.

Listing 4-7 is an excerpt of the full transcript of the episode.

Listing 4-7. The Partial Transcript of Episode 811 of This American Life

```
"...My younger cousin Camille is not really a dog person, but
there is one dog she adored. Her name was Foxy, because she
looked exactly like a fox, except she was black. She was the
neighbor's dog, but she and Camille seemed to have a real
kinship, maybe because they both weren't very far from the
ground. Camille was around four or five years old back then,
and she had a little lisp, so Foxy came out as Fozzie. I
thought it was one of the cutest things I'd ever heard.

The way Camille remembers Foxy, it's almost like a movie. Her
memories feel like endless summer, hazy and perfect, like a
scene shot on crackly film. I just remembered like the feeling
```

of being excited to go and see Foxy. I have an image in my head of like coming to the house, and I could see Foxy was like outside. I can see Foxy through the door that leads to the garden. There's a story about Camille and Foxy that I think about fairly often. I've talked about it with my sister for years, but never with Camille. And it's this. Once when they were playing..."

For brevity, we're only showing an excerpt of the transcript. The full transcript itself is over 8000 words due to the fact that the episode is nearly 1 hr in length.

Going Meta: Prompt Engineering GPT-4 to Write a Prompt for DALL·E

Since the full text transcript of the podcast episode that we want to visualize is thousands of words, we're going to use GPT-4 to automatically create the prompt needed for the DALL·E model. DALL·E is able to take a textual description in a prompt and create an image, but it's best to keep the prompt as short as possible. Listing 4-8 is the prompt for GPT-4 to generate a prompt for DALL·E.

Listing 4-8. The Prompt for GPT-4 to Create a Prompt for DALL·E

System: You are a service that helps to visualize podcasts.
User: Read the following transcript from a podcast. Describe for a visually impaired person the background and subject that best represents the overall theme of the episode. Start with any of the following phrases:
- "A photo of"
- "A painting of"

```
- "A macro 35mm photo of"
- "Digital art of "
```
User: Support for This American Life comes from Squarespace...
Model: gpt-4-32k
Temperature: 1.47
Maximum length: 150
Top P: 0
Frequency penalty: 0.33
Presence penalty: 0

As you can see in the prompt, the model used is the 32k token version of GPT-4 in order to allow us to process REALLY LONG text transcripts. DALL·E needs to know the type of image to generate so that's why we need to specify that the image should be a photo, painting, digital art, etc. We need to ensure that the resulting text generated by GPT-4 is short, so we want to have a maximum length of 150 tokens. Also, in order to prevent GPT-4 from repeating some phrases multiple times, we introduced a frequency penalty of 0.33.

Listing 4-9 shows the results from GPT-4 after reading the transcript of Episode 811 of This American Life.

Listing 4-9. The Prompt for DALL·E Created by GPT-4

```
Digital art of a young girl sitting in a garden with a black
dog that looks like a fox. The girl is smiling and the dog is
wagging its tail. The image has a hazy, dream-like quality,
with crackly film effects to evoke nostalgia.
```

Create Image Endpoint

In order to use the DALL·E model to dynamically create an image from a text prompt, you need to call the **Create Image** Endpoint.

Creating the Request

Table 4-3 lists all the HTTP parameters necessary to call the Create Image Endpoint.

Table 4-3. *The HTTP Parameters Necessary to Call the Create Image Endpoint*

HTTP Param	Description
Endpoint URL	https://api.openai.com/v1/images/generations
Method	POST
Header	Authorization: Bearer **$OPENAI_API_KEY**
Content-Type	application/json

Table 4-4 describes the format of the JSON object necessary for the request body for the Create Image Endpoint. For obvious reasons, the prompt is the only required parameter in order to successfully invoke the service.

Create Image (JSON)

Table 4-4. *Request Body for the Create Image Endpoint*

Field	Type	Required?	Description
prompt	String	Required	This is where you describe the image that you want to be created.
			The maximum length is 1000 characters for dall-e-2 and 4000 characters for dall-e-3.
model	String	Optional	The model name to generate the image.
			Compatible models include • "dall-e-2" • "dall-e-3"
n	integer or null Default: 1	Optional	This is the requested number of images that you want created.
			Must be between 1 and 10.
			Note: Due to the complexity required for dall-e-3, OpenAI may limit your request to a single image.

(continued)

Table 4-4. (*continued*)

Field	Type	Required?	Description
quality	String Default: "standard"	Optional	This allows you to specify the quality of the image to be generated. This parameter is only valid for dall-e-3.
			Accepted values are • "standard" • "hd"
size	String or null Default: "1024x1024"	Optional	The size of the generated images.
			Image sizes available for dall-e-2 are • "256x256" • "512x512" • "1024x1024"
			Image sizes available for dall-e-3 are • "1024x1024" • "1792x1024" (landscape) • "1024x1792" (portrait)

(*continued*)

Table 4-4. (*continued*)

Field	Type	Required?	Description
style	String Default: "vivid"	Optional	This allows you to specify how natural looking the generated image should be. This parameter is only valid for dall-e-3. Accepted values are • "natural" (good for photos) • "vivid" (good for artistic looks)
response_format	String or null Default: "url"	Optional	This is the format of the generated image. Accepted values are • "url" • "b64_json"
user	String	Optional	This is a unique identifier representing your end user, which can help OpenAI to monitor and detect abuse.

Handling the Response

After successfully invoking the Create Image Endpoint, the API will respond with an Image JSON object. Here's a breakdown of the Image object, which only has one parameter (Table 4-5).

Image (JSON)

Table 4-5. *The Structure of the Image JSON Object*

Field	Type	Description
url (or) b64_json	String	This is a url to your generated image if the response_format is "url" in the request. (or) This is a base64-encoded JSON image if the response_format is "b64_json" in the request.

Creating the Image Generator: DALLEClient.java

As you can see from Tables 4-4 and 4-5, the Create Image Endpoint behaves quite similarly to the Chat Endpoint: everything you need to specify to the DALL·E model is encapsulated in a JSON object. Therefore, our code in Listing 4-10 will also use the Jackson library since we'll be working with JSON objects again.

Listing 4-10. Using DALL·E API With Java in DALLEClient.java

```java
import java.io.IOException;

import com.fasterxml.jackson.annotation.JsonProperty;
import com.fasterxml.jackson.databind.ObjectMapper;

import okhttp3.*;

public class DALLEClient {

    public static void main(String[] args) {
```

```java
String openAIKey = "";
String endpoint = "https://api.openai.com/v1/images/
generations";
String contentType = "application/json";
String prompt = "a 35mm macro photo of 3 cute
rottweiler puppies with no collars laying down in
a field";
int numberOfImages = 2;
String size = "1024x1024";

OkHttpClient client = new OkHttpClient();
MediaType mediaType = MediaType.get(contentType);

// Create the Create Image JSON object
CreateImage createImage = new CreateImage(prompt,
numberOfImages, size);

// Use Jackson ObjectMapper to convert the object to
   JSON string
String json = "";
try {
    ObjectMapper mapper = new ObjectMapper();
    json = mapper.writeValueAsString(createImage);
} catch (Exception e) {
    e.printStackTrace();
    return;
}

RequestBody body = RequestBody.Companion.create(json,
mediaType);
Request request = new Request.Builder()
        .url(endpoint)
        .method("POST", body)
        .addHeader("Content-Type", contentType)
```

```java
                .addHeader("Authorization", "Bearer " +
                openAIKey)
                .build();

        try {
            Response response = client.newCall(request).
            execute();
            if (!response.isSuccessful()) throw new
            IOException("Unexpected code " + response);
                System.out.println(response.body().string());
        } catch (Exception e) {
            e.printStackTrace();
        }
    }

    // Inner class for the CreateImage JSON Object
    public static class CreateImage {

        @JsonProperty("prompt")
        private String prompt;

        @JsonProperty("n")
        private int n;

        @JsonProperty("size")
        private String size;

        public CreateImage(String prompt, int n, String size) {
            this.prompt = prompt;
            this.n = n;
            this.size = size;
        }
    }
}
```

Now, since we're already using the OkHttp library to make our HTTP Requests with the Transcriptions Endpoint for the Whisper model, we'll continue to use it for the Create Image Endpoint for the DALL·E model.

The most important thing to understand here is the CreateImage inner class. It has the @JsonProperty annotations, and it encapsulates the important parameters necessary to create an image:

- The text prompt describing the details of the image

- The number of images that you want generated

- The size of the image that you want generated

Figures 4-3 and 4-4 show the image generated from the text prompt in Listing 4-9.

Figure 4-3. *The DALL·E Generated Image of a Girl and Her Dog from Episode 811 of "This American Life" Podcast*

Figure 4-4. *The DALL·E Generated Image of a Girl and Her Dog from Episode 811 of "This American Life" Podcast*

DALL·E Prompt Engineering and Best Practices

Now, creating images with DALL·E takes prompt engineering in order to get consistent, desired results, and it's a good idea to play around with different prompts to get some practice to see what works for you and your use case. Maybe you prefer paintings instead of 3D looking images? Maybe you need photos instead of digital art? Maybe you want the image to be a close-up shot instead of a portrait? There's a lot of possibilities to consider.

Regardless of your use case, here are two golden rules in order to get the most out of your DALL·E prompts.

DALL·E Golden Rule #1: Get Familiar with the Types of Images that DALL·E Can Generate

First and foremost, one of the most important things that DALL·E needs to understand is the type of image that needs to be generated. Here's a list of several of the most common types of images that DALL·E is able to create:

- 3-D render

- Painting

- Abstract painting

- Expressive oil painting

- Oil painting (in the style of any deceased artist)

- Oil pastel

- Digital art

- Photo

- Photorealistic

- Hyperrealistic

- Neon photo

- 35-mm macro photo

- High-quality photo

- Silhouette

- Vaporware

- Cartoon

- Plush object

- Marble sculpture

- Hand sketch

- Poster

- Pencil and watercolor

- Synth wave

- Comic book style

- Hand drawn

DALL·E Golden Rule #2: Be Descriptive with What You Want in the Foreground and Background

I cannot emphasize enough that you need to be descriptive with DALL·E in order to get consistent, desirable results. It may sound weird, but the best way to describe your image to DALL·E is to act like you're describing a dream to another person.

So, as a mental exercise between you and me, try to describe your last dream. As you describe the people, places, and things in your dream, you have in your mind the most important things that you remember, as well as the experience that you felt. As you describe things to another person, tiny details start to emerge such as

- How many people were present (if any)?

- What position were the people or animals in? Standing, sitting, or laying down?

- What things were in the scenery and the background?

- What items stood out to you? Sounds? Smells? Colors?

- How did you feel? Happy, eerie, excited?

- What was the perceived time of day? Morning, midday, night?

If you can describe a dream to another person, then you should have no problem describing what you want to DALL·E.

Conclusion

In this chapter we accomplished a lot! With a few classes we created a Podcast Visualizer.

- We created and used the `AudioSplitter.java` class which works as a utility for us. If you have an audio file that's larger than the limitations of the Whisper model, this class will give you a folder of smaller audio files to send to Whisper.

- We created and used the `WhisperClient.java` class to get a transcription of a folder of audio files. The folder can contain a single audio file or several files. Your only limitation is the number of requests that you can send to the Transcription Endpoint and the Whisper model.

- We did a little prompt engineering with GPT-4 in order to get a descriptive prompt of the imagery in a podcast based upon the transcript.

- Finally, we created and used the `DALLEClient.java` class to take the prompt generated from calling the GPT-4 model and getting an image that represents the podcast episode visually.

Exercises Left for the Reader

So, there are obviously a few additional things we can do here, and these steps will be left for you (the reader) to accomplish, for example:

- The `AudioSplitter.java` app is a Java interface to FFmpeg. FFmpeg can not only split audio files, but can also do a lot more with media files, such as format conversion and reencoding. Experiment to see which of the supported media formats by Whisper are the smallest audio files. Hint: It's definitely not WAV format.

- If you're planning to create an app or a service that automatically generates images based upon a textual prompt from your end users, then you definitely would want to update the `DALLEClient.java` class in order to ensure that you're tracking and providing in your request the user parameter in your HTTP request. This is due to the fact that your end user has the potential to generate harmful images through your API key. Remember, you have an API account with Open AI, and they don't! As a result, you need to be aware if you need to terminate your business relationship with a user who is violating Open AI content rules through your service.

CHAPTER 5

Creating an Automated Community Manager Bot with Discord and Java

When you're launching an app or a service, it's important to build and maintain your own community. Below are the telltale signs of a healthy user community:

- Members engage in meaningful discussions, sharing insights, feedback, and support.

- Disagreements or debates occur, but they are approached constructively without resorting to personal attacks or derogatory language.

- There's an atmosphere of respect, where members listen to each other and acknowledge differing opinions.

© Bruce Hopkins 2024
B. Hopkins, *ChatGPT for Java*, https://doi.org/10.1007/979-8-8688-0116-7_5

- A mix of old and new members actively participate, ensuring the community remains vibrant and doesn't stagnate.

- Users contribute diverse content, from answering questions to sharing resources, which enriches the community's knowledge base.

- There's a balance between giving and taking; members who seek help or information also offer it to others.

- New members frequently join, often referred by existing members, indicating that the community is seen positively and worth recommending.

- Users often become advocates for the community or platform, promoting it outside of the direct community space, such as on social media or other forums.

- The community helps to shape the app or service by providing new ideas for features and functionality.

No matter what type of app or service that I create, I would love for my user community to exemplify the items listed above!

Choosing Discord as Your Community Platform

Over the past few years, Discord has surged in popularity as a useful tool for community management for people who are passionate about their communities. This is partially due to its cross-platform compatibility, allowing members to stay connected whether they're on a desktop, mobile device, or web browser. However, one of its standout features is the invitation-based community system, which helps community managers to control growth and prevents spam. This model not only ensures a tailored experience for members but also enhances security, since community managers have the discretion to grant or deny access.

Discord not only supports text messaging, but also supports voice chats and streaming video. Very similar to Slack, Discord allows community managers to separate content into channels to organize discussions, streamline information flow, and to help users see the content that they're interested in.

Creating a More Advanced Bot Than Our Slack Bot

Now, If you successfully went through the steps in Chapter 3 where we worked with a Slack bot, then the steps in this chapter will feel familiar to you. In Chapter 3, we created a Slack bot to read a single channel during a time period and get a summary of the content discussed. The Slack bot was not a community manager, but was more like a helpful assistant.

For the remainder of this book, we're going to perform all the steps necessary to make powerful bots for Discord that will use AI to help actually manage the community.

Creating a More Advanced Bot Than Any Typical Discord Bot

If you've ever had any experience using a Discord bot, then you're probably aware that the most common way in order to interact with them is with what's called a "/command." This enables typical bots (read: non-intelligent bots) to essentially work only when they have received a very specific operation or command. If the "/command" is not provided, then the bot will be silent and not do anything. Essentially, it exemplifies the phrase, "speak only when you are spoken to."

However, we are creating a Discord bot that will be artificially intelligent, and therefore it will be much more advanced than any typical Discord bot. We're going to create bots that will be able to read and see all messages in the Discord server, and be intelligent enough to respond correctly.

Understanding the Roles for the Bots

So let's explore a scenario in order to make things real. We're creating a public Discord server to interact with the users of a mobile banking app. Our end goal is to have bots written in Java to handle the following scenarios:

- Q&A: Monitor a specific channel and automatically answer questions from users about how to use the banking app. For this to work, the bot will need to be trained on how the app works

- No solicitations: For any business community, it's important that the participants of the community are not being targeted by unscrupulous individuals. For example, if you're creating a banking app, do you want your customers contacted by anyone whose username is "B4nk Admin"?

- No harmful content: For any community, it's important for the members to be protected from harmful content such as hate language.

Our Example Bank: Crook's Bank

For the purposes of this example, I decided upon a fictional name of a fictional bank that would have an extremely low likelihood of coinciding with the name of a real bank. Therefore, for this example, "Crook's Bank" is launching a new mobile app for customers of their bank. They want to have a channel that will be monitored by a bot to answer questions from users of the app, and they also want to ensure that no one is soliciting users of their app, or posting hurtful or harmful content in their Discord servers.

Figure 5-1. *This Fake App from a Fake Bank Has Real Problems*

First Things First: Create Your Own Discord Server

Before we can make an AI Discord Bot, we're obviously going to need a Discord server already in place for the bot to interact with. Use either the Discord App or go to the Discord website (login first of course), and start the process to Add/Create a new server.

After you have started the process, select the option labeled "**Create My Own**" as shown in Figure 5-2.

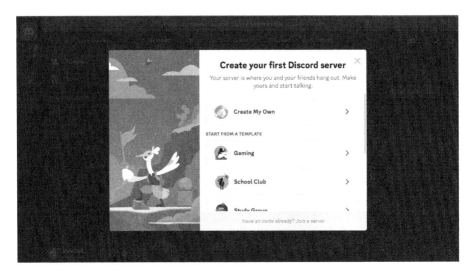

Figure 5-2. *Creating Your Own Discord Server*

Next, you'll be prompted to specify additional information about
your server. Continue to proceed through the creation process until you
are prompted to provide a name and icon for your server, as shown in
Figure 5-3.

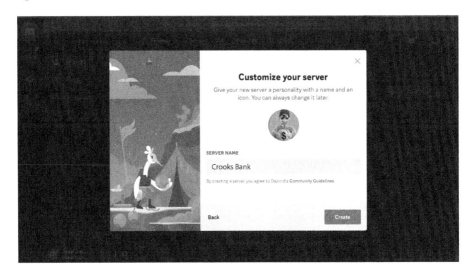

Figure 5-3. *Providing a Name for Your Own Discord Server*

Specify the name of your server and provide an optional server icon (if you have one).

Create the Q&A Channel

By default, every Discord server has a "general" channel, but we want a dedicated channel especially for questions and answers. Depending upon how you created your server, Figure 5-4 and 5-5 will be presented to you to create your new channel.

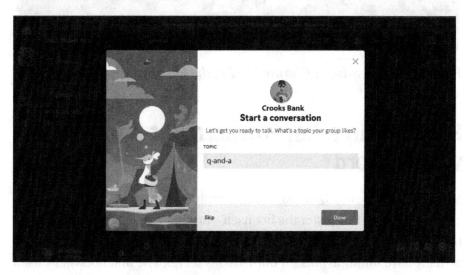

Figure 5-4. *Creating a Channel Using the Web Interface*

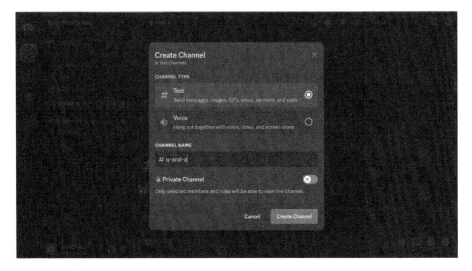

Figure 5-5. *Creating a Channel Using the Discord App*

Registering a New Discord Bot App with Discord

Now that we have our Discord server with the appropriate channels created, it's time to register the bot itself – or rather, in our case, the bots themselves. In order to keep the code clean and manageable, we'll actually have multiple bots for our Discord server. The first bot will be used exclusively to answer questions in the "q-and-a" channel. The second bot will monitor all channels for unwanted content, such as harmful content or solicitations.

In order to create our bot, head over to the Discord Developers website:

https://discord.com/developers

At the top-right of the page, click on the button "**New Application**," as shown in Figure 5-6.

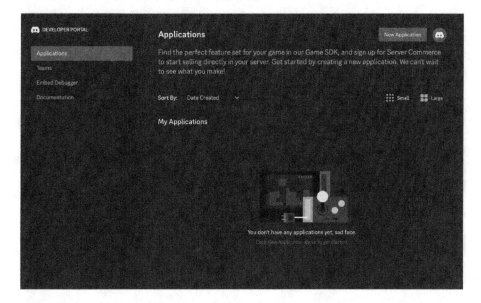

Figure 5-6. *In Order to Create a Discord Bot, Go to the Discord Developer Website*

In both Discord and Slack terminology, a "bot" is an "app," and bots are not allowed to run on Discord servers unless they have been registered with Discord first.

Specify a name for the bot, and click the "**Create**" button, as shown in Figure 5-7.

149

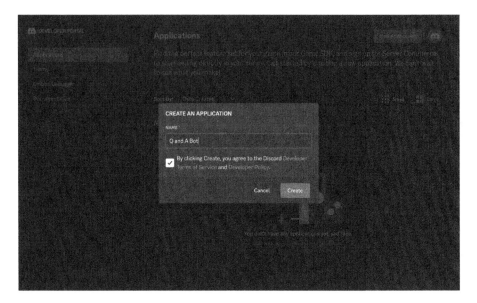

Figure 5-7. *Creating/Registering a Bot for Discord*

Specifying General Info for the Bot

Afterward, you will be taken to a page where you can specify general information about your bot, as shown in Figure 5-8.

Be sure to familiarize yourself with the navigation menu on the left side of the page. As you can see, we have several categories of settings to configure for our bot. By default, we have landed on the "**General Information**" page, where we specify basic info about our bot. If you have an icon ready for your bot, you can upload it here.

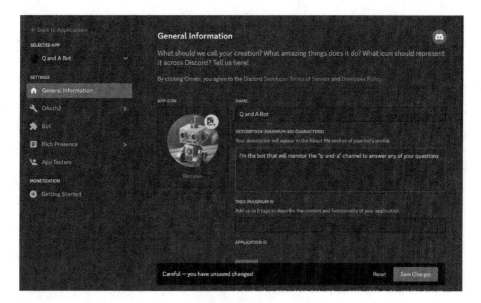

Figure 5-8. *I Decided to Give My Bot a Cute Little Robot Icon*

Specifying OAuth2 Parameters for the Bot

Now it's time to specify the scopes and permissions for our bot. If you followed the steps in creating a Slack bot in Chapter 3, then (as stated before) this procedure will feel familiar to you. Bots **can not** and **should not** have the ability do anything and everything – they should be only allowed to perform a list of operations that they were designed to perform.

On the settings navigation menu on the left, navigate to "**OAuth2 ➤ URL Generator**" to continue.

Below are the scopes that we want:

- Scopes

  - Bot

This is reflected in Figure 5-9.

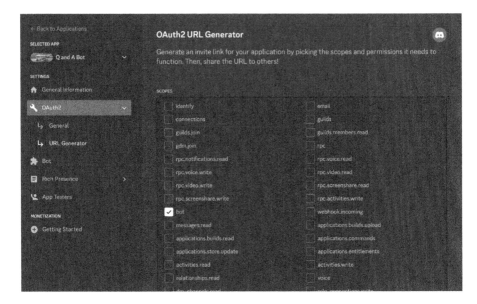

Figure 5-9. *Selecting the Scopes*

After we select the bot's scope, we get to see all the permissions that are only applicable to bots. Bot permissions fall into three categories: **general**, **text**, and **voice**.

In case you're curious about the categories, the general permissions allow the bot to act in the capacity of a normal human moderator, such as managing the server, roles, and channels. Bots with these permissions can also kick and ban members.

Text permissions allow the bot to send and receive messages in text channels, and voice permissions allow the bot to participate in voice channels. Simple enough, right?

Select the following permission for the bot:

- Bot Permissions

  - Text Permissions

    - Send Messages

    - Read Message History

The appropriate permissions are reflected in Figure 5-10.

Figure 5-10. *Selecting the Text Permissions*

Although you haven't written any Java code yet, now it's time to invite your bot to your server.

Invite Your Bot to Your Server

As shown in Figure 5-10, after you have selected the appropriate permissions, Discord will give you a dynamically generated URL that will enable you to invite your bot to your server.

Copy the URL and paste it into a web browser where you're already authenticated into Discord. The result is shown in Figure 5-11.

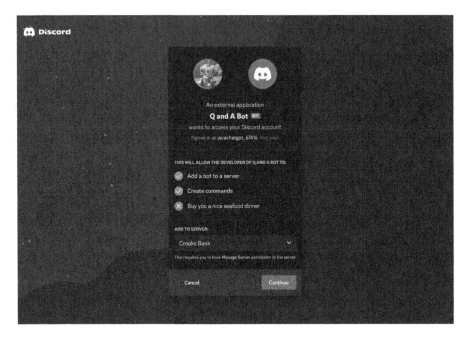

Figure 5-11. *If You Read the Screen Carefully Here, You Can See That Discord Has a Sense of Humor*

Click on the "**Continue**" button to add the bot to your server.

Next, you will see a page that looks quite similar to the previous one, but the main difference is that it will give you a summary of all the permissions and capabilities of the bot. Typically this is quite useful if you are adding a bot to a server that you DID NOT CREATE. However, since we created this bot ourselves, this is just a confirmation of the settings that we have already specified earlier.

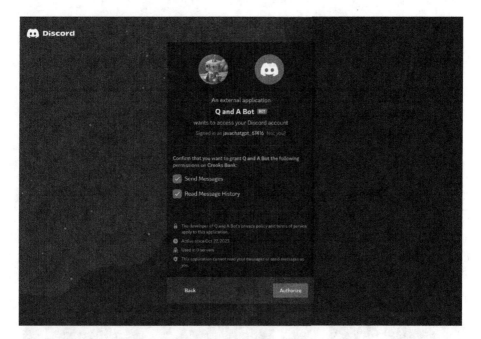

Figure 5-12. *Confirming the capabilities of the bot*

Click the "**Authorize**" button to give the bot the permission to run on your server.

If everything went smoothly, then you should see an automated message in the General channel of your server that indicates that the process has been successful.

Getting the Discord ID Token for Your Bot and Setting the Gateway Intents

Now it's time to get the Discord ID token for your bot, which you'll use in your code to authenticate your bot programmatically.

Note   For obvious reasons, using the word "token" here makes me nervous because this word has two distinct meanings in this book due to the context, but here's a quick refresher on the meanings:

- When using Discord and Slack APIs, a "token" is an authentication token.

- When using OpenAI APIs, a "token" as a part of a word.

Go back to the Discord developer's website, and click the "**Bot**" category in the settings navigation menu to continue.

Although you haven't seen your token yet, you need to click the "Reset Token" button, as shown in Figure 5-13.

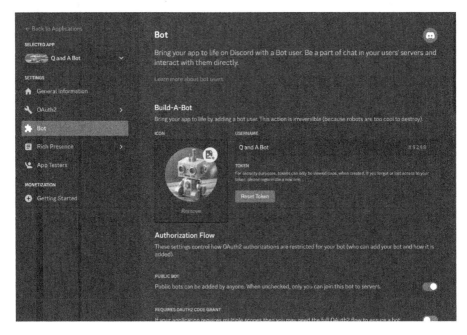

Figure 5-13. *Click the "Reset Token" Button to See Your ID Token*

Be sure to copy and save the ID token to someplace safe. You will need this token in the Java code that's presented later in this chapter.

Scroll down the page to the section named "**Privileged Gateway Intents**," and enable the option named "**MESSAGE CONTENT INTENT.**"

Note   So let's slow things down a bit and talk about intents. What exactly is an "intent" and why is it needed? For the purposes of the Discord API, you need to specify explicitly every type of information that you want to be notified by Discord programmatically. Otherwise, Discord will constantly bombard you with events that are not relevant to you or your bot. For example, for our purposes, we don't care when people join or leave the server. However, if you want to send a list of server rules to anyone who joins your server for the first time, then you definitely would want to enable the "**SERVER MEMBERS INTENT**." When we deep dive into the code, you'll see more information about intents.

Be sure to click the green button, "**Save Changes**," to save your changes. The result is shown in Figure 5-14.

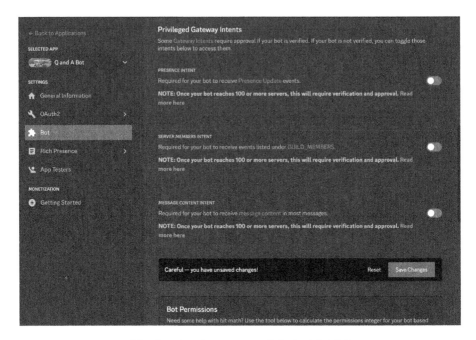

Figure 5-14. *Enable the Option Named "MESSAGE CONTENT INTENT"*

Creating a Q&A Bot App in Java to Answer Questions from a Channel

Of course, now that we've done all the prerequisites necessary and we know the name of the channel that we want to monitor for questions from our users, let's get to the code in Java that joins our server and accesses all the messages from a specific Discord channel.

Setting Up Your Dependencies

The Java Discord API (JDA) library for Java provides developers a very straightforward approach to creating automated apps to work with Discord servers. Mostly everything that we need comes from the net.dv8tion.jda. api package, which exists in the net.dv8tion-<VERSION> jar file.

The JDA library has its own dependencies, which are

- Java Annotations API (this adds support for basic annotations)

    - javax.annotation-api-<VERSION>.jar

- Opus Java (a Java library for real-time audio communication)

    - opus-java-<VERSION>.jar

- Neovisionaries websocket client (a Java library to communicate over web sockets)

    - nv-websocket-client-<VERSION>.jar

- OK HTTP (we're already familiar with this library for HTTP communication)

    - okhttp-<VERSION>.jar

- Apache Commons (a very common library for Java developers)

    - commons-collections4-<VERSION>.jar

- SLF4J (we're already familiar with this library for logging)

    - slf4j-api-<VERSION>.jar

Creating The First Discord Bot: TechSupportBotDumb.java

This is the first of two Discord bots that we're creating in this chapter. This bot, TechSupportBotDumb.java, will be responsible for watching the messages in the "q-and-a" channel in our Discord server.

Later on in this chapter, we'll create another bot that will be responsible for moderating ALL CONTENT in the Discord server for unwanted content, including the "q-and-a" channel. The goal here is to follow the architectural pattern of "separation of concerns." Rather than creating a gigantic Java Discord bot that performs all the moderation needs for the Discord server, we're going to separate the functionality into two different apps.

We're also going to take things step by step and focus this chapter on getting past the learning curve for the Discord capabilities in Java. In the final chapter of this book, we'll enhance both bots and make them artificially intelligent using the Open AI APIs.

Listing 5-1 is the code that we need to create a basic Discord bot that watches all the messages posted in a single channel and provides an answer.

Listing 5-1. TechSupportBotDumb.java

```
import java.io.IOException;
import java.util.EnumSet;

import net.dv8tion.jda.api.JDA;
import net.dv8tion.jda.api.JDABuilder;
import net.dv8tion.jda.api.entities.Activity;
import net.dv8tion.jda.api.entities.User;
import net.dv8tion.jda.api.entities.channel.ChannelType;
import net.dv8tion.jda.api.events.message.MessageReceivedEvent;
```

```java
import net.dv8tion.jda.api.hooks.ListenerAdapter;
import net.dv8tion.jda.api.requests.GatewayIntent;

// This class extends a ListenerAdapter to handle message
events on Discord.
public class TechSupportBotDumb extends ListenerAdapter {

    // The bot's Discord token for authentication.
    static String discordToken = "YOUR_DISCORD_BOT_TOKEN";
    // The name of the channel the bot should monitor and
    interact with.
    static String channelToWatch = "q-and-a";

    public static void main(String[] args) throws IOException {

        // Set of intents declaring which types of events the
        bot intends to listen to.
        EnumSet<GatewayIntent> intents = EnumSet.of(
                GatewayIntent.GUILD_MESSAGES, // For messages
                in guilds.
                GatewayIntent.DIRECT_MESSAGES, // For private
                direct messages.
                GatewayIntent.MESSAGE_CONTENT // To allow
                access to message content.
        );

        // Initialize the bot with minimal configuration and
        the specified intents.
        try {
            JDA jda = JDABuilder.createLight(discordToken,
            intents)
                        .addEventListeners
                        (new TechSupportBotDumb()) // Adding the
                        current class as an event listener.
```

```
                    .setActivity(Activity.customStatus
                    ("Ready to answer questions")) // Set the
                    bot's custom status.
                    .build();

            // Asynchronously get REST ping from Discord API
            and print it.
             jda.getRestPing().queue(ping ->   System.out.
             println("Logged in with ping: " + ping) );
            // Block the main thread until JDA is fully loaded.
            jda.awaitReady();

            // Print the number of guilds the bot is
            connected to.
            System.out.println("Guilds: " + jda.
            getGuildCache().size());
        } catch (InterruptedException e) {
            // Handle exceptions if the thread is interrupted
            during the awaitReady process.
            e.printStackTrace();
        }
    }

    // This method handles incoming messages.
    @Override
    public void onMessageReceived(MessageReceivedEvent
    messageEvent) {
        // The ID of the sender.
        User senderDiscordID = messageEvent.getAuthor();

        // Ignore messages sent by the bot to prevent self-
        responses.
```

```
    if (senderDiscordID.equals(messageEvent.getJDA().
    getSelfUser())) {
        return;
    } else if (messageEvent.getChannelType() ==
    ChannelType.TEXT) {
        // Ignore messages not in the specified "q-and-a"
        channel.
        if (!messageEvent.getChannel().getName().equalsIgno
        reCase(channelToWatch)) {
            return;
        }
    }
    // Send a greeting response to the user who sent the
    message.
    String reply = "hi <@" + senderDiscordID.getId() + ">,
    I can help you with that!";
    messageEvent.getChannel().sendMessage(reply).queue();
    }
}
```

In our class, we need to extend the ListenerAdapter class from the JDA API in order to get things to work. Now, as you analyze TechSupportBotDumb.java, you should see that we kept things really simple, and therefore we only have two methods to worry about: main() and onMessageReceived().

At beginning of the class, you should also notice that we specify the channel that we are interested in monitoring with the "channelToWatch" variable.

> **Note** For some reason, Discord's own terminology sometimes refers to Discord servers as "guilds." Therefore, the JDA library will also use the word, guild, when referring to a Discord server. However, from our perspective, a guild is simply a Discord server.

In the main() method we have a Collection (specifically, it's an EnumSet, but at the end of the day, it's still a Collection) of GatewayIntents. As you may remember, you use Intents to specify explicitly the type of information that you're interested in. In our case, we're interested in

- Messages sent to the server (guild messages)

- Messages sent directly to the bot from a user (direct messages)

- The content of the messages sent (message content)

Afterward, we again use the Builder Pattern with the JDABuilder class with our discordToken and the intents that we're interested in with the following call:

```
JDA jda = JDABuilder.createLight(discordToken, intents)
```

Loving the Lambda Expression to Simplify Code

Within the main() method, we're using a Lambda expression to send a ping request to the Discord servers using the JDA library asynchronously. Like all network requests, if this is not done asynchronously, then our main thread will be blocked until the response is received, which is a bad thing. Therefore, after the ping response is received, we execute the println() statement to show how long the ping request takes to get to the server. Using a Java Lambda expression, this is accomplished using

```
jda.getRestPing().queue(ping ->  System.out.println("Logged in
with ping: " + ping) );
```

So what if we didn't use a Lambda expression to get the ping time to Discord's servers? The code would look more like this:

```
// instantiate a new PingConsumer
jda.getRestPing().queue(new PingConsumer());
...
// define the PingConsumer as an inner class
class PingConsumer implements Consumer<Long> {
    @Override
    public void accept(Long ping) {
        System.out.println("Logged in with ping: " + ping);
    }
}
```

Without the Lambda, we'd need to create an inner class implementing the Consumer interface (which honestly, we don't really care about). By implementing the interface, we need to implement the accept() method, which will be asynchronously called when the response comes back. We would then create a new PingConsumer instance in the jda.getRestPing(). queue() method call.

Handling Messages Sent to the Discord Server

As we wrap things up for this first Java Discord bot, we need to talk about the onMessageReceived() method. This method is called asynchronously for every single message the Discord server, as well as for messages from users sent directly to the bot itself as a DM.

> **Note**   Did you know that when the bot sends an answer to a person's question in the Discord server, Discord will invoke the onMessageReceived() method of the bot to give the bot the message that the bot just sent. This sounds like a recipe for an infinite loop, doesn't it? Therefore, we have logic in place for the bot to ignore messages sent from itself.

In the final lines of the onMessageReceived() method, we make sure that we give a friendly reply to the original sender of the message by "@ tagging" them in the response. As we mentioned before, this first version of the Q&A Bot is dumb. It will respond to your question when posted in the Discord server, but the response won't actually answer your question.

Success! Running Your First Discord Bot: TechSupportBotDumb.java

Figure 5-15. *Success Running the Q&A Bot in Discord*

Now let's run our Java Discord bot. After executing the app, be sure to return back to your Discord server, and try to type a question in the channel that you setup for Q&A. Figure 5-15 shows the response to my question, "Is this bot going to answer my questions about the app?"

As you carefully inspect Figure 5-15, you'll see some key features such as

- On the right side, you'll see that the bot is online with a green status indicator.

- The bot also has a custom status to let you know what it will do in the channel.

- After asking a question in the channel, the bot will tag you directly.

Streamlining the Process of Registering Our Next Discord Bot App with Discord

Now that we have successfully performed all the steps in order to get a functioning Discord bot, creating the second bot will be a piece of cake! So, let's briefly reiterate all the steps from above in order to create our second Discord bot. I'll make sure to point out the items that need to be changed or enhanced due to the fact that this second bot will work as a moderator, instead of providing answers to questions from the users of our Discord server.

Registering a New Discord Bot App with Discord

Perform the same steps as above; however, it would be wise to give the bot a different name. For me, this second bot will be named "Content Mod Bot."

Specifying General Info for the Bot

For me, I have a different icon for the Content Moderator bot, so I specified it here (Figure 5-16).

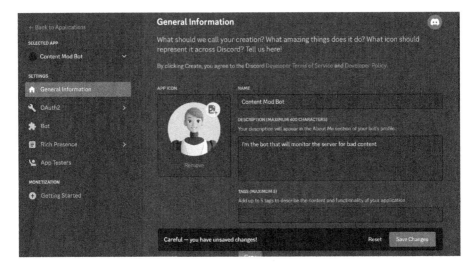

Figure 5-16. *Providing a Name and Icon for the Second Bot*

Specifying OAuth2 Parameters for the Bot

This second bot needs more permissions in order to perform more tasks. Below are the scopes that we want:

- Scopes

  - Bot

Select the following permission for the bot:

- Bot Permissions

  - General Permissions

    - Kick Members

    - Ban Members

- Text Permissions

  - Send Messages

  - Manage Messages

  - Read Message History

Invite Your Bot to Your Server

Repeat the same steps as above for the first bot.

Getting the Discord ID Token for Your Bot and Setting the Gateway Intents

Again, follow the steps above in order to get the Discord ID Token. Then scroll down the page to the section named "**Privileged Gateway Intents**," and enable the options named "**SERVER MEMBERS INTENT**" and "**MESSAGE CONTENT INTENT**."

Creating the Next Discord Bot: ContentModeratorBotDumb.java

The role of the content moderator is to make sure that unwanted content is not posted in the Discord server. Just like the previous bot that we created earlier in this chapter, this bot will not (yet) be artificially intelligent. In its current state, the bot will indiscriminately delete any message posted anywhere in the server that contains the word "puppies."

It's not because puppies are inherently evil. However, they do have a tendency to destroy your favorite pair of shoes when left alone. In all honesty, we simply need something to test our code in Discord when we run our bot.

Listing 5-2 is the code for ContentModeratorBotDumb.java.

Listing 5-2. ContentModeratorBotDumb.java

```java
import java.io.IOException;
import java.util.EnumSet;

import net.dv8tion.jda.api.JDA;
import net.dv8tion.jda.api.JDABuilder;
import net.dv8tion.jda.api.entities.Activity;
import net.dv8tion.jda.api.entities.Message;
import net.dv8tion.jda.api.entities.User;
import net.dv8tion.jda.api.entities.channel.unions.
MessageChannelUnion;
import net.dv8tion.jda.api.events.message.MessageReceivedEvent;
import net.dv8tion.jda.api.hooks.ListenerAdapter;
import net.dv8tion.jda.api.requests.GatewayIntent;

// This class extends a ListenerAdapter to handle message
events on Discord.
public class ContentModeratorBotDumb extends ListenerAdapter {

    // The bot's Discord token for authentication.
    static String discordToken = "YOUR_DISCORD_BOT_TOKEN";
    static String bannedWord = "puppies";

    public static void main(String[] args) throws IOException {
```

```java
// Set of intents declaring which types of events the
bot intends to listen to.
EnumSet<GatewayIntent> intents = EnumSet.of(
        GatewayIntent.GUILD_MEMBERS,    // to get access
        to the members of the Discord server
        GatewayIntent.GUILD_MODERATION, // to ban and
        unban members
        GatewayIntent.GUILD_MESSAGES, // For messages
        in guilds
        GatewayIntent.MESSAGE_CONTENT // To allow
        access to message content
);

// Initialize the bot with minimal configuration and
the specified intents.
try {
    JDA jda = JDABuilder.createLight(discordToken,
    intents)
            .addEventListeners(new
            ContentModeratorBotDumb()) // Adding the
            current class as an event listener.
            .setActivity(Activity.customStatus("Helping
            to keep a friendly Discord server")) // Set
            the bot's custom status.
            .build();

    // Asynchronously get REST ping from Discord API
    and print it.
    jda.getRestPing().queue(ping -> System.out.
    println("Logged in with ping: " + ping));

    // Block the main thread until JDA is fully loaded.
    jda.awaitReady();
```

```
        // Print the number of guilds the bot is
        connected to.
        System.out.println("Guilds: " + jda.
        getGuildCache().size());
        // Print the Discord userID of the bot
        System.out.println("Bot's ID: " + jda.
        getSelfUser());
    } catch (InterruptedException e) {
        // Handle exceptions if the thread is interrupted
        during the awaitReady process.
        e.printStackTrace();
    }
}

@Override
public void onMessageReceived(MessageReceivedEvent
messageEvent){

    User senderDiscordID = messageEvent.getAuthor();
    MessageChannelUnion channel = messageEvent.
    getChannel();
    Message message = messageEvent.getMessage();

    // Check whether the message was sent in a guild
    / server
    if (messageEvent.isFromGuild()){

        String content = message.getContentDisplay();
        // Check if the message contains the banned word
        if (content.contains(bannedWord)){
```

```
            // Delete the message
            message.delete().queue();

            // Mention the user who sent the
            inappropriate message
            String authorMention = senderDiscordID.
            getAsMention();

            // Send a message mentioning the user and
            explaining why it was inappropriate
            channel.sendMessage(authorMention + " This
            comment was deemed inappropriate for this
            channel. " +
                    "If you believe this to be in error,
                    please contact one of the human server
                    moderators.").queue();
        }

     }
  }
}
```

Handling Messages Sent to the Discord Server

Again, let's focus our attention on the onMessageReceived() method, since
it's called asynchronously every time a message is posted to the Discord
server. As you can see, if the message posted to the server contains the
banned word, then we delete the message, and warn the sender with a
@mention message in the same channel where the offending message
was posted.

Success Again! Running Your Second Discord Bot: ContentModeratorBotDumb.java

Now let's run our second Java Discord bot. After executing the app, be sure to return back to your Discord server, and type a message in any channel that contains the offending word. Figure 5-17 shows the bot in action.

Figure 5-17. *This Bot Has a Strict Rule About Discussing "Puppies"; However, Discussing "Kittens" Is Perfectly Fine*

Conclusion

We just went through all the steps necessary to create two functioning Discord bots in Java. For those who are unfamiliar with the process of creating a Discord server, we showed the process on how to setup a server to manage our community.

As you can see, we took a much different approach compared to our Slack bot that we did in Chapter 3! The Slack bot that we created was pretty much focused on user productivity within the workplace. The two Discord bots, on the other hand, are truly focused on community management. We have everything in place for these bots to be artificially intelligent with the help of OpenAI's APIs. This is all accomplished in the final two chapters.

Exercises Left for the Reader

In the next chapter we're going to make our "dumb" bots to be intelligent, but there's at least one thing we can do right now. Rather than using the command line to report status messages, it's better for the bots to have their own channel that's exclusively used for status reports. This way, when the bot starts up, shuts down, or has anything important to inform the administrators, it's all logged and recorded in a central location.

CHAPTER 6

Adding Intelligence to Our Discord Bots, Part 1: Using the Chat Endpoint for Q&A

At this point, we have all the structure in place to make both our Discord bots that we created in the previous chapter to be fully functional and artificially intelligent. In the last two chapters of this book, we're going to follow all the steps necessary in order to make both bots to be artificially intelligent. In this chapter, we'll get started with our Tech Support Bot, which was called TechSupportBotDumb.java. Below are the two major changes that we're going to make:

- Modify our ChatGPTClient.java class so that the Discord bot class can ask questions about specific information that we provide to it. The updated class will be called ChatGPTClientForQAandModeration. java. It will be used for Q&A purposes in this chapter but will be used in the final chapter of the book as well.

© Bruce Hopkins 2024
B. Hopkins, *ChatGPT for Java*, https://doi.org/10.1007/979-8-8688-0116-7_6

- Modify our TechSupportBot.java class (formerly
  named TechSupportBotDumb.java) so that it can load
  an external text file that contains frequently asked
  questions with the answers. TechSupportBot.java
  will then provide the contents of the text file to the
  ChatGPTClientForQAandModeration.java class who
  is responsible for creating the prompt and of course
  invoking the Chat Endpoint.

Making TechSupportBot.java More Intelligent

Listing 6-1 contains the full contents of the frequently asked questions
that the fictional customer support team has created based upon support
tickets from users of the newly launched mobile banking application.

Listing 6-1. FAQ.txt

```
1. What is the Crooks Bank Mobile App?
The Crooks Bank Mobile App is a cutting-edge mobile banking app
that allows you to manage your finances, make transactions, and
access a wide range of banking services conveniently from your
mobile device.

2. How can I download the Crooks Bank Mobile App?
You can download the Crooks Bank Mobile App from the App
Store for iOS devices and Google Play for Android devices.
Simply search for the "Crooks Bank Mobile App" and click the
"Install" button.
```

3. Is the Crooks Bank Mobile App safe and secure?
Yes, the Crooks Bank Mobile App prioritizes your security. We use
state-of-the-art encryption and security protocols to protect
your data and transactions. Your information is safe with us.

4. What features does the Crooks Bank Mobile App offer?
The Crooks Bank Mobile App provides a variety of features,
including:

- Account Management: View account balances, transaction
  history, and more.
- Transfer Funds: Easily transfer money between your
  accounts or to other bank accounts.
- Bill Payments: Pay bills and manage recurring payments.
- Deposit Checks: Snap photos of checks for remote deposit.
- ATM Locator: Find nearby ATMs and branches.
- Notifications: Receive alerts for account activity and
  important updates.

5. Can I link external accounts to the Crooks Bank Mobile App?
Yes, the Crooks Bank Mobile App supports linking external
accounts from other financial institutions. You can monitor and
manage your accounts from different banks in one place.

6. How can I reset my password if I forget it?
If you forget your password, simply click the "Forgot Password"
option on the login screen. You'll receive instructions on how
to reset your password.

7. What are the fees associated with the Crooks Bank
Mobile App?
The Crooks Bank Mobile App aims to be transparent with its
fees. You can find information on account fees, transaction
charges, and other costs in the "Fees" section within the app
or on our website.

8. Can I get customer support through the Crooks Bank
Mobile App?
Absolutely! We offer customer support through our in-app
messaging feature. You can also find our customer service
contact information on our website.

9. Is the Crooks Bank Mobile App available for business
accounts?
The Crooks Bank Mobile App primarily caters to personal banking
needs. However, we have plans to introduce business banking
services in the future.

10. How can I provide feedback or suggestions for the Crooks
Bank Mobile App?
We welcome your feedback! You can submit suggestions and
feedback through the "Contact Us" section in the app or on our
website.

As you can see in the Frequently Asked Questions text file in Listing 6-1, there's no magic involved here. It's simply a list of questions and the answers. Now, let's see the newly modified TechSupportBot.java class. This is represented in Listing 6-2.

Listing 6-2. TechSupportBot.java

```java
import java.io.BufferedReader;
import java.io.FileReader;
import java.io.IOException;
import java.util.EnumSet;

import net.dv8tion.jda.api.JDA;
import net.dv8tion.jda.api.JDABuilder;
import net.dv8tion.jda.api.entities.Activity;
import net.dv8tion.jda.api.entities.User;
```

```java
import net.dv8tion.jda.api.entities.channel.ChannelType;
import net.dv8tion.jda.api.entities.channel.unions.
MessageChannelUnion;
import net.dv8tion.jda.api.events.message.MessageReceivedEvent;
import net.dv8tion.jda.api.hooks.ListenerAdapter;
import net.dv8tion.jda.api.requests.GatewayIntent;

// This class extends a ListenerAdapter to handle message
events on Discord.
public class TechSupportBot extends ListenerAdapter {

    // The bot's Discord token for authentication.
    static String discordToken = "";
    // The name of the channel the bot should monitor and
    interact with.
    static String channelToWatch = "q-and-a";
    // Variable to store FAQ contents
    static String contentsFromFAQ = "";
    static String pathToFAQFile = "/Users/Desktop/FAQ.txt";
    // the system message
    static String systemMessage = "You are a virtual assistant
    that provides support for the Crooks Bank banking app. ".";
    // our ChatGPT client
    static ChatGPTClientForQAandModeration
    chatGPTClient = null;

    public static void main(String[] args) throws IOException {

        // Set of intents declaring which types of events the
        bot intends to listen to.
        EnumSet<GatewayIntent> intents = EnumSet.of(
                GatewayIntent.GUILD_MESSAGES, // For messages
                in guilds.
```

```
        GatewayIntent.DIRECT_MESSAGES, // For private
        direct messages.
        GatewayIntent.MESSAGE_CONTENT // To allow
        access to message content.
);

// Read the contents of an external text file into
FAQContents variable
contentsFromFAQ = readFileContents(pathToFAQFile);

// create a new ChatGPTClientForQAandModeration
chatGPTClient = new ChatGPTClientForQAandModeration(con
tentsFromFAQ, systemMessage);

// Initialize the bot with minimal configuration and
the specified intents.
try {
    JDA jda = JDABuilder.createLight(discordToken,
    intents)
            .addEventListeners(new TechSupportBot())
            // Adding the current class as an event
            listener.
            .setActivity(Activity.customStatus("Ready
            to answer questions")) // Set the bot's
            custom status.
            .build();

    // Asynchronously get REST ping from Discord API
    and print it.
    jda.getRestPing().queue(ping -> System.out.
    println("Logged in with ping: " + ping));

    // Block the main thread until JDA is fully loaded.
    jda.awaitReady();
```

```java
        // Print the number of guilds the bot is
        connected to.
        System.out.println("Guilds: " + jda.
        getGuildCache().size());
        System.out.println("Self user: " + jda.
        getSelfUser());
    } catch (InterruptedException e) {
        // Handle exceptions if the thread is interrupted
        during the awaitReady process.
        e.printStackTrace();
    }
}

// This method handles incoming messages.
@Override
public void onMessageReceived(MessageReceivedEvent
messageEvent) {

    // The ID of the sender
    User senderDiscordID = messageEvent.getAuthor();
    // The Discord channel where the message was posted
    MessageChannelUnion channel = messageEvent.
    getChannel();
    net.dv8tion.jda.api.entities.Message message =
    messageEvent.getMessage();
    String reply = null;

    // Ignore messages sent by the bot to prevent self-
    responses.
    if (senderDiscordID.equals(messageEvent.getJDA().
    getSelfUser())) {
        return;
```

```java
        } else if (messageEvent.getChannelType() ==
        ChannelType.TEXT) {
            // Ignore messages not in the specified "q-and-a"
            channel.
            if (!channel.getName().equalsIgnoreCase(channelT
            oWatch)) {
                return;
            }
        }

        // Show "typing" status while the bot is working
        channel.sendTyping().queue();

        // this line takes the question from the Discord users
        and asks ChatGPT
        reply = chatGPTClient.sendMessageFromDiscordUser
        (message.getContentDisplay());
        channel.sendMessage(reply).queue();
    }

    // New method to read file contents
    private static String readFileContents(String filePath) {
        try (BufferedReader reader = new BufferedReader
        (new FileReader(filePath))) {
            StringBuilder content = new StringBuilder();
            String line;
            while ((line = reader.readLine()) != null) {
                content.append(line).append("\n");
            }
            return content.toString();
        } catch (IOException e) {
            e.printStackTrace();
            return "Failed to read FAQ contents.";
```

```
            }
        }
    }
```

Important Changes to Note from the Previous Version of the Tech Support Bot

Let's briefly analyze TechSupportBot.java and discuss the changes that were made. The following code snippet contains a portion of the class definition section.

```
static String contentsFromFAQ = "";
static String pathToFAQFile = "/Users/Desktop/FAQ.txt";
static String systemMessage = "You are a virtual assistant
that provides support for the Crooks Bank banking app. ";
static ChatGPTClientForQAandModeration
chatGPTClient = null;
```

As you can see, we're defining some Strings that provide a reference to the file path location where the frequently asked questions file is stored. We also have a String that will be used to contain the contents of the file itself.

Now, as we have learned from the previous chapters in the book, you can dramatically set the tone of the conversation by providing a specific message to the system itself in your prompt. Therefore, we have a String here as well containing the system message. Finally, we have a reference to a Class, ChatGPTClientForQAandModeration, which will be quite similar to the other ChatGPTClient classes that we use previously in the book.

Updates to the onMessageReceived() Method

Now, when a message is received, be sure to notice the following line:

```
net.dv8tion.jda.api.entities.Message message = messageEvent.
getMessage();
```

Here, we need to give the full package and class name of the Message class used by the JDA library because we already created and use a Message class for encapsulating and representing the JSON objects when we send HTTP requests to the Chat Endpoint.

Now let's further examine the following three lines of code:

```
channel.sendTyping().queue();
reply = chatGPTClient.sendMessageFromDiscordUser(message.
getContentDisplay());
channel.sendMessage(reply).queue();
```

Here, we provide a nice user experience and show the user that the bot is "typing," while the user's question is being sent to ChatGPT. When the response comes back, we provide the reply back to the user.

Analyzing ChatGPTClientForQAandModeration.java

In Listing 6-2, TechSupportBot.java instantiates ChatGPTClientForQAandModeration.java which (as we stated previously) is very similar to the ChatGPTClient classes we have used before. The complete source for ChatGPTClientForQAandModeration.java is shown in Listing 6-3.

Listing 6-3. ChatGPTClientForQAandModeration.java

```java
import com.fasterxml.jackson.core.JsonProcessingException;
import com.fasterxml.jackson.databind.JsonNode;
import com.fasterxml.jackson.databind.ObjectMapper;

import java.io.BufferedReader;
import java.io.IOException;
import java.io.InputStreamReader;
import java.io.OutputStream;
import java.net.HttpURLConnection;
import java.net.URL;
import java.util.ArrayList;
import java.util.List;

public class ChatGPTClientForQAandModeration {

    //
    //  OpenAI parameters that we already know how to use
    //
    String openAIKey = "";
    String endpoint = "https://api.openai.com/v1/chat/
    completions";
    String model = "gpt-4";
    float temperature = 1.0f;
    int max_tokens = 256;
    float top_p = 1.0f;
    int frequency_penalty = 0;
    int presence_penalty = 0;

    String systemMessage = null;
    String initialInstructionsToChatGPT = null;
```

```
    //
    // The constructor needs to be passed the contents from the
    FAQ.txt file
    // and the system message
    //
    public ChatGPTClientForQAandModeration(String
    systemMessage, String initialInstructionsToChatGPT) {
        this.systemMessage = systemMessage;
        this.initialInstructionsToChatGPT =
        initialInstructionsToChatGPT;
    }

    public String sendMessageFromDiscordUser(String
    discordMessageText) {

        String answerFromChatGPT = "";

        List<Message> messages = new ArrayList<>();
        messages.add(new Message("system", systemMessage));
        messages.add(new Message("user",
        initialInstructionsToChatGPT));
        messages.add(new Message("user", discordMessageText));

        String jsonInput = null;
        try {
            ObjectMapper mapper = new ObjectMapper();

            Chat chat = Chat.builder()
                .model(model)
                .messages(messages)
                .temperature(temperature)
                .maxTokens(max_tokens)
                .topP(top_p)
```

```
        .frequencyPenalty(frequency_penalty)
        .presencePenalty(presence_penalty)
        .build();

    jsonInput = mapper.writeValueAsString(chat);
    System.out.println(jsonInput);
} catch (JsonProcessingException e) {
    e.printStackTrace();
}

try {
    URL url = new URL(endpoint);
    HttpURLConnection connection = (HttpURLConnection)
    url.openConnection();
    connection.setRequestMethod("POST");
    connection.setRequestProperty("Content-Type",
    "application/json");
    connection.setRequestProperty("Authorization",
    "Bearer " + openAIKey);
    connection.setDoOutput(true);

    OutputStream outputStream = connection.
    getOutputStream();
    outputStream.write(jsonInput.getBytes());
    outputStream.flush();
    outputStream.close();

    int responseCode = connection.getResponseCode();
    if (responseCode == HttpURLConnection.HTTP_OK) {
        BufferedReader reader = new BufferedReader(new
        InputStreamReader(connection.
        getInputStream()));
        StringBuilder response = new StringBuilder();
```

```java
            String line;
            while ((line = reader.readLine()) != null) {
                response.append(line);
            }
            reader.close();

            // Print the response
            answerFromChatGPT =
            extractAnswerFromJSON(response.toString());
            System.out.println(answerFromChatGPT);
        } else {
            System.out.println("Error: " + responseCode);
        }
        connection.disconnect();
    } catch (IOException e) {
        e.printStackTrace();
    }
    return answerFromChatGPT;
}

//
// We are only interested in the "message.content" in the
JSON response
// So here's the easy way to extract that
//
public String extractAnswerFromJSON(String jsonResponse) {
    String chatGPTAnswer = "";

    try {
        // Create an ObjectMapper instance
        ObjectMapper objectMapper = new ObjectMapper();

        // Parse the JSON string
```

```
JsonNode rootNode = objectMapper.
readTree(jsonResponse);

// Extract the "content" parameter
JsonNode contentNode = rootNode.at("/choices/0/
message/content");
chatGPTAnswer = contentNode.asText();

System.out.println("Content: " + chatGPTAnswer);

} catch (Exception e) {
    e.printStackTrace();
}

return chatGPTAnswer;
    }
}
```

One of the most important things to note is that in the constructor, we are sending the full String of the contents of the frequently asked questions as well as the message that we're going to be providing to the system itself.

```
public ChatGPTClientForQAandModeration(String
knowledgeBaseFileContents, String systemMessage) {
        this.knowledgeBaseFileContents =
        knowledgeBaseFileContents;
        this.systemMessage = systemMessage;
    }
```

This way, after we have constructed the ChatGPTClientForQAandModeration.java class, we can reuse the object already constructed in order to ask the individual questions from our users.

Every time a question has been posted on our Discord channel, TechSupportBot.java will call sendMessageFromDiscordUser() from ChatGPTClientForQAandModeration.java. In this method, we will perform all of the usual things necessary in order to invoke the Chat Endpoint.

Using JSONPath in Order to Extract Content Quickly in JSON Files

Sometimes, it can be a little messy writing the code necessary in order to extract a single node within a JSON file. Therefore, I wrote a simple method using JSONPath in order to extract the "message.content" node in the resulting JSON file returned by the Chat Endpoint. It's all performed with this single line of code:

```
JsonNode contentNode = rootNode.at("/choices/0/message/
content");
```

In my opinion, JSONPath is pretty efficient in order to extract a single node or group of nodes from within a JSON file, but the expressions themselves and the syntax necessary can be as daunting to read as regular expressions. So, if you've never used JSONPath before, or if you need help on how to write the expressions, then pair-program with ChatGPT!

Running Our Intelligent Q&A Bot: TechSupportBot.java

Now let's run our new and improved Q&A Java Discord bot, TechSupportBot.java. After executing the app, be sure to return back to your Discord server, and start asking questions. Figure 6-1 shows the bot in action.

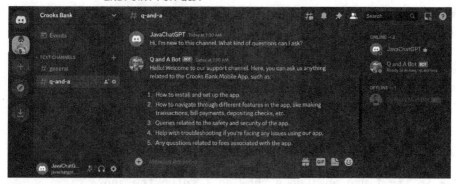

Figure 6-1. *Having a Discussion with Our Intelligent DISCORD Q&A BOT, TechSupportBot.java*

Listing 6-4 shows the conversation between us and the Discord Bot.

Listing 6-4. Our First Conversation with the Intelligent Q&A Discord Bot

Me: Hi, I'm new to this channel. What kind of questions can I ask?

Q and A Bot: Hello! Welcome to our support channel. Here, you can ask us anything related to the Crooks Bank Mobile App, such as:

1. How to install and set up the app.
2. How to navigate through different features in the app, like making transactions, bill payments, depositing checks, etc.
3. Queries related to the safety and security of the app.
4. Help with troubleshooting if you're facing any issues using our app.
5. Any questions related to fees associated with the app.
Don't hesitate to ask us anything else related to our services! We're here to assist you.

Me: I have an old Blackberry phone, is the app supported on
my device?

Q and A Bot: I'm sorry for the inconvenience, but at the
moment, the Crooks Bank Mobile App is currently only available
for iOS and Android devices. It is not supported on Blackberry
or any other operating systems. You may still manage your bank
accounts by accessing our website through your phone's browser.

Me: So, if I use an iPhone, how do I setup the app?

Q and A Bot: Sure, here's how you can set up the Crooks Bank
Mobile App on your iPhone:

1. Open the App Store on your iPhone.
2. In the search bar at the top, type in "Crooks Bank Mobile
App" and tap "Search".
3. Once you can see the app in the search results, simply tap
on the "Get" button to download it.
4. After the app downloads, tap "Open".
5. You'll have to agree to our Terms and Conditions upon the
first launch.
6. If you're an existing Crooks Bank member, you can log in
using your online banking user ID and password. If you're a new
member, you'll need to register for an account.
7. Once you're logged in, you can set up Touch ID or Face ID
for quicker, secure login in the future.
8. Now you can start using your Crooks Bank Mobile App to
manage your finances, pay bills, make transactions, and more!

Please make sure you update the app regularly to access new
features and improvements. If you have any challenges during
setup, please reach out to us through the app's support feature
or call our customer service.

We Have a Monumental Achievement... With One Slight Flaw

OK, if you step back and examine what we have achieved so far, you should realize that we're looking at what is nothing short of a monumental achievement. We have the following:

- A system made up of a few classes that allows users to type in questions and get answers about how to use our mobile application.

- Using a simple text file, we can teach our bot how to answer the questions from our users. This can be edited by anyone in the company and can be used as a knowledge base to help improve the intelligence of the bot day by day. This is amazing stuff.

- The system allows customers to type their questions using natural language, and the bot provides an intelligent answer back to them. Guess what? Customers don't like reading FAQs - especially really long ones. However, using this system, they don't need to! All they have to do is ask the question that is relevant to them.

So, with all this that we have accomplished, there's one GIGANTIC flaw that we can't ignore. In Listing 6-4, the bot said to the user:

```
Once you're logged in, you can set up Touch ID or Face ID for
quicker, secure login in the future.
```

No, no, no! Bad bot! In case you didn't read the frequently asked questions file completely, please allow me to explain what went wrong here:

1. The FAQ.txt file in Listing 6-1 clearly states that the Crooks Bank mobile app is a mobile app. Currently, Touch ID can only be used on Apple desktop and laptop computers. So this doesn't even make sense.

2. The FAQ.txt file has no mention of Face ID for authentication to the mobile app at all.

So unfortunately, ChatGPT is making up things that are simply not true and is assuming that certain features exist that are not present. So, for the purposes of true tech support, this is absolutely unacceptable.

So, how do we solve this? Think about how you could solve this problem for a second before reading the next section.

Update the System Message to ChatGPT and Let's Try Again

Have you come up with a solution yet? One way to resolve this issue is to update the System Message. Refer to the following line in Listing 6-2:

```
static String systemMessage = "You are a virtual assistant that
provides support for the Crooks Bank banking app. ";
```

Remember that the System Message indicates to ChatGPT what it's role is in the chat conversation. Right now it is told to be a helpful assistant, and therefore, it has taken the liberty in order to guess that certain features exist within the mobile application. Now, let's ensure that ChatGPT does not provide any assumptions. Update the System Message to be as shown here:

```
static String systemMessage = "You are a virtual assistant
that provides support for the Crooks Bank banking app. You
will be provided Information about the application, and users
will ask you questions about the application. Your role is to
```

answer questions explicitly from the training information. If
you were not given an answer to a question, then provide an
apologetic message to the user explaining that you do not know
the answer.";

And that's it. The FAQ.txt file remains exactly the same as before, and
all we needed to do is to update the System Message to let ChatGPT know
it's role in the conversation. Listing 6-5 has the new conversation between
us and the Discord bot.

Listing 6-5. Our Second and Better Conversation with the
Intelligent Q&A Discord Bot

Me: How are you today?

Q and A Bot: As a virtual assistant, I don't have feelings or
emotions, but I'm here and ready to assist you. How may I help
you with the Crooks Bank Mobile App today?

Me: I have an old Blackberry phone, is the app supported on
my device?

Q and A Bot: I'm sorry, but from the information provided, the
Crooks Bank Mobile App can only be downloaded from the App
Store for iOS devices and Google Play for Android devices.
BlackBerry devices are not mentioned, therefore I cannot
confirm that it would be compatible.

Me: So, if I use an iPhone, how do I setup the app?

Q and A Bot: To set up the Crooks Bank Mobile App on your iPhone,
you can download it from the App Store. Simply search for "Crooks
Bank Mobile App" and click the "Install" button. After the
installation is finished, open the app and follow the prompts to
set up your account. If you already have an account, use your
login information to access your account through the app.

Now that's a lot better! Our Tech Support bot is "sticking to the script" and is not allowed to makeup or assume anything.

Conclusion

In this chapter, we've accomplished a lot! We have a fully functioning Discord bot that can be trained by anyone without any experience in AI, NLP, or Machine Learning using a simple text file. We learned that a "helpful assistant" may at times become TOO HELPFUL and assume facts that are not true. However, we also reiterated the concept and the value of the System Message, which is an important part of Prompt Engineering.

Now that we have made our Q&A Discord bot to be intelligent, now let's find out how to make out Content Moderator bot to be intelligent as well!

Adding Intelligence to Our Discord Bots, Part 2: Using the Chat and Moderation Endpoints for Moderation

In this chapter, we're going to take the steps necessary in order to make our Content Moderator Discord bot artificially intelligent. Let's overview the changes that we're going to make:

- Create a new class, ModerationClient.java, to invoke the Moderations Endpoint. The Moderations Endpoint allows us to be aware when any textual content fits any of the following categories:

  - Hate

  - Hate/threatening

- Harassment

- Harassment/threatening

- Self-harm

- Self-harm/intent

- Self-harm/instructions

- Sexual

- Sexual/minors

- Violence

- Violence/graphic

- Reuse our ChatGPTClientForQAandModeration.java
  from the previous chapter. In Chapter 6, it was used
  to invoke the Chat Endpoint for Q&A purposes from
  our users. In this chapter, it will be used to invoke the
  Chat Endpoint again, but this time for moderation
  purposes. This is why the class is aptly named.
  "ChatGPTClientForQAandModeration," because it's
  used for Q&A in Chapter 6, but also for moderation in
  this chapter.

- Modify our ContentModeratorBot.java class (formerly
  named ContentModeratorBotDumb.java) so that
  it can invoke both the ModerationClient.java and
  ChatGPTClientForQAandModeration.java. If either
  classes indicate that the content typed in the Discord
  channel is objectionable, then delete the message from
  that Discord channel. Remember, this bot watches all
  content in all channels of the Discord server!

Note   Now, it this point, you may be asking yourself, if the
Moderations Endpoint already knows how to flag any harmful
content, then why do we need to use Chat Endpoint as well? Good
question.

Yes, the Moderations Endpoint will allow us to know about harmful
content, but it **DOES NOT** inform us about any other types of unwanted
content for our scenario, such as when unscrupulous individuals try to lure
our users into a scam. Remember, this is a Discord server for a banking
app, so scammers would definitely love to target all the members of this
Discord server since it's a central location full of bank users!

Therefore, we'll use the ModerationClient.java to invoke the
Moderations Endpoint to know if any content in the Discord server is
harmful, and we'll reuse the ChatGPTClientForQAandModeration.java
from the last chapter in order to invoke the Chat Endpoint in order to be
made aware of any other undesirable content is posted in the Discord
server, such as scam attempts.

Moderations Endpoint

The Moderations Endpoint allows developers to submit a String of text,
and to subsequently know if it's violent, hateful, threatening, or contains
any form of harassment.

Creating the Request

Table 7-1 lists all the HTTP parameters necessary to call the Moderations Endpoint.

Table 7-1. *The HTTP Parameters for the Moderations Endpoint*

HTTP Param	Description
Endpoint URL	`https://api.openai.com/v1/moderations`
Method	POST
Header	Authorization: Bearer **$OPENAI_API_KEY**
Content-Type	`application/json`

Table 7-2 describes the format of the JSON object necessary for the request body for the Moderations Endpoint. The service is very simple to use, since only one parameter is required to properly invoke the service.

Create Moderation (JSON)

Table 7-2. *The Request Body for the Moderation Endpoint*

Field	Type	Required?	Description
Input	String or Array	Required	The text that needs to be classified.
Model	String default: "text-moderation-latest"	Optional	There are actually two content moderation models available for use: "text-moderation-stable" and "text-moderation-latest."
			By default, this is set to "text-moderation-latest." It will be automatically upgraded over time, which ensures you're always using the most accurate model.
			If you use "text-moderation-stable," you will be given advance notice before the model is updated.
			The accuracy of "text-moderation-stable" tends to be slightly lower than for "text-moderation-latest."

Handling the JSON Response

After successfully invoking the Moderations Endpoint, the service will provide a JSON response with the structure shown in Table 7-3.

Moderation (JSON)

Table 7-3. *The Structure of the Moderation JSON Object*

Field	Type	Description
Id	String	A unique identifier for the moderation request.
Model	String	The model used to perform the moderation request.
Results	Array	A list of moderation objects.
↳ flagged	Boolean	Flags if the content violates OpenAI's usage policies.
↳ categories	Array	A list of the categories and whether they're being flagged or not.
↳↳ hate	Boolean	This indicates whether or not the text given expresses, incites, or promotes hate based on race, gender, religion, ethnicity, nationality, disability status, sexual orientation, or caste.
↳↳ hate/ threatening	Boolean	This indicates whether or not the text given contains hateful content that also threatens violence or serious harm toward the targeted group based on biases expressed above.
↳↳ harassment	Boolean	This indicates whether or not the text given contains content that expresses, incites, or promotes harassing language toward any target.
↳↳ harassment/ threatening	Boolean	This indicates whether or not the text given contains harassment content that also threatens violence or serious harm toward any target.
↳↳ self-harm	Boolean	This indicates whether or not the text given contains content that promotes, encourages, or depicts acts of self-harm, for example, suicide, cutting, and eating disorders.

(continued)

Table 7-3. (*continued*)

Field	Type	Description
↳↳ self-harm/ intent	Boolean	This indicates whether or not the text given contains content in which the speaker expresses that they are engaging or intend to engage in acts of self-harm, such as suicide, cutting, and eating disorders.
↳↳ self-harm/ instructions	Boolean	This indicates whether or not the text given contains content that encourages the performing acts of self-harm, such as suicide, cutting, and eating disorders. This includes content that gives instructions or advice on how to commit such acts.
↳↳ sexual	Boolean	This indicates whether or not the text given contains content meant to arouse sexual excitement, such as the description of sexual activity. This includes content that promotes sexual services; however, this ***excludes*** topics such as sex education and wellness.
↳↳ sexual/ minors	Boolean	This indicates whether or not the text given contains content that includes an individual under the age of 18.
↳↳ violence	Boolean	This indicates whether or not the text given contains content depicting death, violence, or physical injury.
↳↳ violence/ graphic	Boolean	This indicates whether or not the text given contains content depicting death, violence, or physical injury in graphic detail.
↳ category_ scores	Array	A list of the categories along with the scores given by the model.
↳↳ hate	Number	Score for the category "hate."

(*continued*)

Table 7-3. (*continued*)

Field	Type	Description
↳↳ hate/threatening	Number	Score for the category "hate/threatening."
↳↳ harassment	Number	Score for the category "harassment."
↳↳ harassment/threatening	Number	Score for the category "harassment/threatening."
↳↳ self-harm	Number	Score for the category "self-harm."
↳↳ self-harm/intent	Number	Score for the category "self-harm/intent."
↳↳ self-harm/instructions	Number	Score for the category "self-harm/instructions."
↳↳ sexual	Number	Score for the category "sexual."
↳↳ violence	Number	Score for the category "violence."
↳↳ violence/graphic	Number	Score for the category "violence/graphic."

Listing 7-1 is an example of the JSON response after invoking the
Moderation Endpoint. Table 7-3 looks a little complex, but as you can see,
if any of the categories is labeled as "true" then the **results.flagged** node is
labeled as "true."

Take a look at Listing 7-1 for a practical example of the Moderation
JSON object.

Listing 7-1. The Moderation JSON Object

```
{
  "id": "modr-XXXXX",
  "model": "text-moderation-005",
  "results": [
      {
      "flagged": true,
      "categories": {
      "sexual": false,
      "hate": false,
      "harassment": false,
      "self-harm": false,
      "sexual/minors": false,
      "hate/threatening": false,
      "violence/graphic": false,
      "self-harm/intent": false,
      "self-harm/instructions": false,
      "harassment/threatening": true,
      "violence": true,
      },
      "category_scores": {
      "sexual": 1.2282071e-06,
      "hate": 0.010696256,
      "harassment": 0.29842457,
      "self-harm": 1.5236925e-08,
      "sexual/minors": 5.7246268e-08,
      "hate/threatening": 0.0060676364,
```

```
      "violence/graphic": 4.435014e-06,
      "self-harm/intent": 8.098441e-10,
      "self-harm/instructions": 2.8498655e-11,
      "harassment/threatening": 0.63055265,
      "violence": 0.99011886,
      }
      }
  ]
}
```

Creating Our Client for the Moderations Endpoint: ModerationClient.java

Listing 7-2 is our client to invoke the Moderations Endpoint. Take a look at it, and then we'll discuss the important parts afterward.

Listing 7-2. ModerationClient.java

```java
import com.fasterxml.jackson.core.JsonProcessingException;
import com.fasterxml.jackson.databind.JsonNode;
import com.fasterxml.jackson.databind.ObjectMapper;

import java.io.BufferedReader;
import java.io.IOException;
import java.io.InputStreamReader;
import java.io.OutputStream;
import java.net.HttpURLConnection;
import java.net.URL;
import java.util.ArrayList;

public class ModerationClient {
```

```java
// OpenAI parameters that we already know how to use
String openAIKey = "";
String endpoint = "https://api.openai.com/v1/moderations";
String model = "text-moderation-latest";

// The constructor
public ModerationClient() {
}

public ModerationResponse checkForObjectionalContent(String
discordMessageText) {

    ModerationResponse moderationResponse = null;

    String jsonInput = null;
    try {
        ObjectMapper mapper = new ObjectMapper();

        ModRequest modRequest = new
        ModRequest(discordMessageText, model);

        jsonInput = mapper.writeValueAsString(modRequest);
        System.out.println(jsonInput);
    } catch (JsonProcessingException e) {
        e.printStackTrace();
    }

    try {
        URL url = new URL(endpoint);
        HttpURLConnection connection = (HttpURLConnection)
        url.openConnection();
        connection.setRequestMethod("POST");
        connection.setRequestProperty("Content-Type",
        "application/json");
```

```
connection.setRequestProperty("Authorization",
"Bearer " + openAIKey);
connection.setDoOutput(true);

OutputStream outputStream = connection.
getOutputStream();
outputStream.write(jsonInput.getBytes());
outputStream.flush();
outputStream.close();

int responseCode = connection.getResponseCode();
if (responseCode == HttpURLConnection.HTTP_OK) {
    BufferedReader reader = new BufferedReader
    (new InputStreamReader(connection.
    getInputStream()));
    StringBuilder response = new StringBuilder();
    String line;
    while ((line = reader.readLine()) != null) {
        response.append(line);
    }
    reader.close();

    // Print the response
    //System.out.println(response.toString());
    // Extract the answer from JSON
    moderationResponse = getModerationResponsefrom
    JSON(response.toString());
    String answerFromChatGPT = moderationResponse.
    toString();
    System.out.println(answerFromChatGPT);
} else {
    System.out.println("Error: " + responseCode);
}
```

```java
            connection.disconnect();
        } catch (IOException e) {
            e.printStackTrace();
        }
        return moderationResponse;
    }

    public ModerationResponse getModerationResponsefromJSON
    (String jsonResponse) {
        ModerationResponse response = new ModerationResponse();
        ObjectMapper mapper = new ObjectMapper();
        try {
            JsonNode rootNode = mapper.readTree(jsonResponse);
            JsonNode resultsNode = rootNode.path("results");
            if (!resultsNode.isMissingNode() && resultsNode.
            isArray() && resultsNode.size() > 0) {
                JsonNode resultNode = resultsNode.get(0);
                response.isFlagged = resultNode.
                path("flagged").asBoolean(false);
                JsonNode categoriesNode = resultNode.
                path("categories");
                if (!categoriesNode.isMissingNode()) {
                    categoriesNode.fields().
                    forEachRemaining(entry -> {
                        if (entry.getValue().
                        asBoolean(false)) {
                            response.offendingCategories.
                            add(entry.getKey());
                        }
                    });
                }
            }
```

```
        } catch (JsonProcessingException e) {
            e.printStackTrace();
        }
        return response;
    }

    class ModerationResponse {
        boolean isFlagged = false;
        ArrayList<String> offendingCategories = new
        ArrayList<>();

        @Override
        public String toString() {
            return "ModerationResponse{" +
                    "isFlagged=" + isFlagged +
                    ", offendingCategories=" +
                    offendingCategories +
                    '}';
        }
    }

}
```

Since in the previous chapters in this book, we created clients for
other Endpoints for the OpenAI API, the class above should look quite
familiar. However, at the end of the class, we have an inner class named
ModerationResponse.

```
    class ModerationResponse {
        boolean isFlagged = false;
        ArrayList<String> offendingCategories = new
        ArrayList<>();
```

This class encapsulates the valuable information from the Moderation JSON object which is returned from the Moderations Endpoint. Namely, if the original Discord message that we want evaluated violates the content rules, we have a boolean, isFlagged, to let us know. If isFlagged is true, then offendingCategories is populated with the categories that the content has been flagged for.

Therefore, the method getModerationResponsefromJSON() does exactly what the name says. We pass the Moderation JSON object returned by the Moderations Endpoint, and we get a fully instantiated ModerationResponse object.

Making ContentModeratorBot.java More Intelligent

Now that we have ModerationClient.java to invoke the Moderations Endpoint, let's take a look at the updated ContentModeratorBot. java (formerly named ContentModeratorBotDumb.java) that will use the ModerationClient.java to check for harmful content and the ChatGPTClientForQAandModeration.java (unmodified from the previous chapter) to check for potential scams.

Listing 7-3 is the full source code for our intelligent Discord Moderator Bot, ContentModeratorBot.java.

Listing 7-3. ContentModeratorBot.java

```
import java.io.IOException;
import java.util.EnumSet;

import net.dv8tion.jda.api.JDA;
import net.dv8tion.jda.api.JDABuilder;
import net.dv8tion.jda.api.entities.Activity;
import net.dv8tion.jda.api.entities.User;
```

```java
import net.dv8tion.jda.api.entities.channel.unions.
MessageChannelUnion;
import net.dv8tion.jda.api.events.message.MessageReceivedEvent;
import net.dv8tion.jda.api.hooks.ListenerAdapter;
import net.dv8tion.jda.api.requests.GatewayIntent;

// This class extends a ListenerAdapter to handle message
events on Discord.
public class ContentModeratorBot extends ListenerAdapter {

    // The bot's Discord token for authentication.
    static String discordToken = "";

    // the system message
    // This is a Java 13+ Multiline String notation. At the end
    of the day, it's still a String
    static String systemMessage = """
        You are the automated moderator assistant for a
        Discord server.
        Review each message for the following rule violations:
        1. Sensitive information
        2. Abuse
        3. Inappropriate comments
        4. Spam, for example; a message in all capital
           letters, the same phrase or word being repeated
           over and over, more than 3 exclamation marks or
           question marks.
        5. Advertisement
        6. External links
        7. Political messages or debate
        8. Religious messages or debate
```

If any of these violations are detected, respond with
"FLAG" (in uppercase without quotation marks). If the
message adheres to the rules, respond with "SAFE" (in
uppercase without quotation marks).
""";

```java
static String instructionsToChatGPT = "Analyze the
following message for rule violations:";

// this is our Chat Endpoint client
static ChatGPTClientForQAandModeration
chatGPTClient = null;
// this is our Moderations Endpoint client
static ModerationClient moderationClient = null;

public static void main(String[] args) throws IOException {

    // Set of intents declaring which types of events the
    bot intends to listen to.
    EnumSet<GatewayIntent> intents = EnumSet.of(
            GatewayIntent.GUILD_MEMBERS,    // to get access
            to the members of the Discord server
            GatewayIntent.GUILD_MODERATION, // to ban and
            unban members
            GatewayIntent.GUILD_MESSAGES, // For messages
            in guilds
            GatewayIntent.MESSAGE_CONTENT // To allow
            access to message content
    );

    // create a new ChatGPTClientForQAandModeration
    chatGPTClient = new ChatGPTClientForQAandModeration
    (systemMessage, instructionsToChatGPT);
```

```java
// create a new ModerationClient
moderationClient = new ModerationClient();

// Initialize the bot with minimal configuration and
the specified intents.
try {
    JDA jda = JDABuilder.createLight(discordToken,
    intents)
            .addEventListeners(new
            ContentModeratorBot()) // Adding the
            current class as an event listener.
            .setActivity(Activity.customStatus("Helping
            to keep a friendly Discord server")) // Set
            the bot's custom status.
            .build();

    // Asynchronously get REST ping from Discord API
    and print it.
    jda.getRestPing().queue(ping -> System.out.
    println("Logged in with ping: " + ping));

    // Block the main thread until JDA is fully loaded.
    jda.awaitReady();

    // Print the number of guilds the bot is
    connected to.
    System.out.println("Guilds: " + jda.
    getGuildCache().size());
    // Print the Discord userID of the bot
    System.out.println("Bot's ID: " + jda.
    getSelfUser());
} catch (InterruptedException e) {
```

```java
        // Handle exceptions if the thread is interrupted
        during the awaitReady process.
        e.printStackTrace();
    }
}

@Override
public void onMessageReceived(MessageReceivedEvent
messageEvent){

    String chatGPTResponse = "";
    ModerationClient.ModerationResponse
    moderationResponse = null;
    User senderDiscordID = messageEvent.getAuthor();

    // The Discord channel where the message was posted
    MessageChannelUnion channel = messageEvent.
    getChannel();
    net.dv8tion.jda.api.entities.Message message =
    messageEvent.getMessage();

    // Ignore messages sent by the bot to prevent self-
    responses.
    if (senderDiscordID.equals(messageEvent.getJDA().
    getSelfUser())) {
        return;
    }

    // this line takes the message from the Discord user
    and invokes the Moderation Endpoint
    moderationResponse = moderationClient.checkForObjection
    alContent(message.getContentDisplay());

    // this line takes the message from the Discord user
    and invokes the Chat Endpoint
```

```java
        chatGPTResponse = chatGPTClient.sendMessageFromDiscordU
        ser(message.getContentDisplay());

        // Check whether the message was sent in a guild
        / server
        if (messageEvent.isFromGuild()){

            // Check both the Chat Endpoint and Moderation
            Endpoint to see if the message is flagged

            if (chatGPTResponse.equals("FLAG") ||
            moderationResponse.isFlagged ){

                // Delete the message
                message.delete().queue();

                // Mention the user who sent the
                inappropriate message
                String authorMention = senderDiscordID.
                getAsMention();

                // Send a message mentioning the user and
                explaining why it was inappropriate
                channel.sendMessage(authorMention + " This
                comment was deemed inappropriate for this
                channel. " +
                        "If you believe this to be in error,
                        please contact one of the human server
                        moderators.").queue();
            }

        }

    }

}
```

Important Changes to Note from the Previous Version of the Content Moderator Bot

Let's briefly take a look at ContentModeratorBot.java from Listing 7-3 and discuss the changes that were made. The following code snippet contains a portion of the class definition section.

```
static String systemMessage = """
        You are the automated moderator assistant for a
        Discord server.
        Review each message for the following rule violations:
        1. Sensitive information
        2. Abuse
        3. Inappropriate comments
        4. Spam, for example; a message in all capital
           letters, the same phrase or word being repeated
           over and over, more than 3 exclamation marks or
           question marks.
        5. Advertisement
        6. External links
        7. Political messages or debate
        8. Religious messages or debate

        If any of these violations are detected, respond with
        "FLAG" (in uppercase without quotation marks). If the
        message adheres to the rules, respond with "SAFE" (in
        uppercase without quotation marks).
        """;

    static String instructionsToChatGPT = "Analyze the
    following message for rule violations:";
```

```
// this is our Chat Endpoint client
static ChatGPTClientForQAandModeration
chatGPTClient = null;
// this is our Moderation Endpoint client
static ModerationClient moderationClient = null;
```

If you're using Java 13+, then you can define a whole block of text using "triple quote" notation. This is how we defined the System Message that will be used by the ChatGPTClientForQAandModeration class.

Updates to the onMessageReceived( ) Method

After a message is received in any channel of the Discord server, the onMessageReceived() method is invoked. Here's the most important change to be aware of:

```
moderationResponse = moderationClient.checkForObjection
alContent(message.getContentDisplay());

chatGPTResponse = chatGPTClient.sendMessageFromDiscord
User(message.getContentDisplay());

// Check whether the message was sent in a guild
/ server
if (messageEvent.isFromGuild()){

    // Check both the Chat Endpoint and Moderation
    Endpoint to see if the message is flagged

    if (chatGPTResponse.equals("FLAG") ||
    moderationResponse.isFlagged ){

        // Delete the message
        message.delete().queue();
```

```
// Mention the user who sent the
inappropriate message
String authorMention = senderDiscordID.
getAsMention();

// Send a message mentioning the user and
explaining why it was inappropriate
channel.sendMessage(authorMention + " This
comment was deemed inappropriate for this
channel. " +
        "If you believe this to be in error,
        please contact one of the human server
        moderators.").queue();
}
```

Here, we take each message that was posted in the Discord server and
check it with both the Moderations Endpoint and the Chat Endpoint. If
either Endpoints return to inform us that the message is flagged, then we
delete the message in the channel and inform the user that their message
violated the rules.

Now that our Content Moderator Discord bot is intelligent, let's give
it a try!

Running Our Intelligent Content Moderator Bot: ContentModeratorBot.java

Now let's run our new and improved Content Moderator Java Discord bot,
ContentModeratorBot.java. After executing the app, be sure to return back
to your Discord server, and start asking questions. Figure 7-1 shows the bot
in action.

Figure 7-1. *Having a Discussion with Our Intelligent DISCORD
Content Moderator Bot: ContentModeratorBot.java*

Listing 7-4 shows a conversation between us and the Discord Bot in
order to test to see what it can do.

Listing 7-4. Our Offensive Conversation with the Intelligent
Moderator Discord Bot

Me: Hi everyone, I love the Crooks Bank app!

Me: This app is awesome! 🤗

Me: Come to my website! http://www.google.com

Content Mod Bot: @JavaChatGPT This comment was deemed
inappropriate for this channel. If you believe this to be in
error, please contact one of the human server moderators.

Me: I'm sorry for breaking the rules. I'm a different
person now

Me: But I have some sad news for you

Me: I want to 💀 everyone

Content Mod Bot: @JavaChatGPT This comment was deemed inappropriate for this channel. If you believe this to be in error, please contact one of the human server moderators.

In both cases when unwanted content was posted in any channel of the Discord server, not only was the offending user called out, but the bad message was deleted. Good bot!

Did you notice that the Moderation and Chat Endpoints are able to read emojis as well?

Conclusion

In this chapter, we created a fully functioning content moderator for our entire Discord server! We leveraged both the Moderations and Chat Endpoints from OpenAI to create a custom content moderator that not only flags unsafe content like hateful and threatening messages, but also prevents the users of the Discord server from being subject to unwanted solicitations.

Exercises Left for the Reader

Although we accomplished a lot in this chapter (as well as in this book!), there's still one more thing that we can do to improve the code. For example:

- The individual Discord bots that we created are aware to not respond to messages that they send themselves. However, the bots are not yet aware that they shouldn't respond to messages sent by **OTHER BOTS**. In other words, if you run both bots at the same time, and someone posts something bad in the "q-and-a" channel, the Content Moderator will, of course, delete

the message and inform everyone that the message was
deleted. However, since the Tech Support Bot doesn't
know that it shouldn't respond to other bots, it will try
to create a response. Of course, bots should not talk to
other bots.

APPENDIX 1

List of OpenAI Models

After executing the code in Listing 2-3, ListModels.java, you will be presented with a JSON object that has a list of the OpenAI models available to you. The following table shows a snapshot of the response.

ID	Object	Created	Owned By
ada	model	1649357491	openai
ada-code-search-code	model	1651172505	openai-dev
ada-code-search-text	model	1651172510	openai-dev
ada-search-document	model	1651172507	openai-dev
ada-search-query	model	1651172505	openai-dev
ada-similarity	model	1651172507	openai-dev
babbage	model	1649358449	openai
babbage-002	model	1692634615	system
babbage-code-search-code	model	1651172509	openai-dev
babbage-code-search-text	model	1651172509	openai-dev
babbage-search-document	model	1651172510	openai-dev
babbage-search-query	model	1651172509	openai-dev
babbage-similarity	model	1651172505	openai-dev
canary-tts	model	1699492935	system

(continued)

© Bruce Hopkins 2024
B. Hopkins, *ChatGPT for Java*, https://doi.org/10.1007/979-8-8688-0116-7

ID	Object	Created	Owned By
canary-whisper	model	1699656801	system
code-davinci-edit-001	model	1649880484	openai
code-search-ada-code-001	model	1651172507	openai-dev
code-search-ada-text-001	model	1651172507	openai-dev
code-search-babbage-code-001	model	1651172507	openai-dev
code-search-babbage-text-001	model	1651172507	openai-dev
curie	model	1649359874	openai
curie-instruct-beta	model	1649364042	openai
curie-search-document	model	1651172508	openai-dev
curie-search-query	model	1651172509	openai-dev
curie-similarity	model	1651172510	openai-dev
dall-e-2	model	1698798177	system
davinci	model	1649359874	openai
davinci-002	model	1692634301	system
davinci-instruct-beta	model	1649364042	openai
davinci-search-document	model	1651172509	openai-dev
davinci-search-query	model	1651172505	openai-dev
davinci-similarity	model	1651172509	openai-dev
gpt-3.5-turbo	model	1677610602	openai
gpt-3.5-turbo-0301	model	1677649963	openai
gpt-3.5-turbo-0613	model	1686587434	openai
gpt-3.5-turbo-1106	model	1698959748	system
gpt-3.5-turbo-16k	model	1683758102	openai-internal

(continued)

ID	Object	Created	Owned By
gpt-3.5-turbo-16k-0613	model	1685474247	openai
gpt-3.5-turbo-instruct	model	1692901427	system
gpt-3.5-turbo-instruct-0914	model	1694122472	system
gpt-4	model	1687882411	openai
gpt-4-0314	model	1687882410	openai
gpt-4-0613	model	1686588896	openai
gpt-4-1106-preview	model	1698957206	system
gpt-4-vision-preview	model	1698894917	system
text-ada-001	model	1649364042	openai
text-babbage-001	model	1649364043	openai
text-curie-001	model	1649364043	openai
text-davinci-001	model	1649364042	openai
text-davinci-002	model	1649880484	openai
text-davinci-003	model	1669599635	openai-internal
text-davinci-edit-001	model	1649809179	openai
text-embedding-ada-002	model	1671217299	openai-internal
text-search-ada-doc-001	model	1651172507	openai-dev
text-search-ada-query-001	model	1651172505	openai-dev
text-search-babbage-doc-001	model	1651172509	openai-dev
text-search-babbage-query-001	model	1651172509	openai-dev
text-search-curie-doc-001	model	1651172509	openai-dev
text-search-curie-query-001	model	1651172509	openai-dev
text-search-davinci-doc-001	model	1651172505	openai-dev

(continued)

ID	Object	Created	Owned By
text-search-davinci-query-001	model	1651172505	openai-dev
text-similarity-ada-001	model	1651172505	openai-dev
text-similarity-babbage-001	model	1651172505	openai-dev
text-similarity-curie-001	model	1651172507	openai-dev
text-similarity-davinci-001	model	1651172505	openai-dev
tts-1	model	1681940951	openai-internal
tts-1-1106	model	1699053241	system
tts-1-hd	model	1699046015	system
tts-1-hd-1106	model	1699053533	system
whisper-1	model	1677532384	openai-internal

Index

A, B

Application programming
    interfaces (APIs),
    see OpenAI
Artificial intelligence (AI)
    ChatGPTClientForQAand
      Moderation.java, 186–194
    FAQ.txt file, 196
    moderations endpoint, 199
    monumental achievement, 195
    onMessageReceived()
      method, 186
    TechSupportBot.java class,
      178–186
    See also Multimodal AI
AudioSplitter.java, 111–116, 123,
    125, 127, 140
Automatic Speech Recognition
    (ASR), 102–108

C

Chat Generation Pre-Trained
    Transformer (ChatGPT), 1
    analysis information, 7–9
    data model, 11
    factory pattern, 4
    Java design patterns, 3

    language models, 2
    neural network, 10
    observer pattern, 4
    OpenAI (*see* OpenAI)
    pre-trained model, 11
    regular expressions, 6–8
    response, 3
    singleton pattern, 3
    string tokenizer, 15, 16
    temperature, 17
    token counter, 46, 47
ChatGPT, *see* Chat Generation
    Pre-Trained Transformer
    (ChatGPT)
ChatGPTClientForQAand
    Moderation.java
    JSONPath, 192
    source code, 186–194
    TechSupportBot.java, 192–198
ChatGPTClient.Java, 48
    builder pattern, 58, 60–63
    Chat Object, 58–60
    initial conversation, 48, 49
    Message.java class, 63
    resulting code, 54–56
    source code, 49–54
Community management
    app/service, 141

Community management (*cont.*)
   Discord (*see* Discord bot)
   Slack bot, 143
ContentModeratorBotDumb.
   java, 170–174
ContentModeratorBot.java, 221–223
   class definition, 219–221
   onMessageReceived() method,
     220, 221
   source code, 213–221

D

DALL·E model, 12, 100, 101
   create image endpoint
     HTTP parameters, 128
     JSON object, 132
     request body, 129–131
     response handling, 131
   DALLEClient.java class,
     132–136, 140
   GPT-4, 126–132
   prompt engineering, 136–139
     common types, 137, 138
     descriptive, 138, 139
   text prompt, 135
Discord bot
   authorize button, 155
   capabilities, 155
   channel creation, 147, 148
   "/command", 143
   community platform, 142, 143
   ContentModeratorBotDumb.
     java, 170–174

ContentModeratorBot.
   java, 221–224
continue button, 154–156
creation/registering app, 150
Crook's Bank, 144, 145
dependencies, 159
developers website, 148–150
general info, 168
general information page,
   150, 151
ID token, 155–158
intelligent (*see* Artificially
   intelligent (AI))
JDA library, 159
message content intent, 158
OAuth2 parameters, 151–153,
   168, 169
onMessageReceived()
   method, 173
privileged gateway intents, 169
registering bot app, 167
scenarios, 144
server, 145, 146, 169
system message, 196–198
TechSupportBotDumb.
   java, 160–167
TechSupportBot.java, 193
text permissions, 153–155
web interface, 147

E, F

Embeddings model, 13
eXtreme Programming (XP), 25

G, H

Generative Pre-trained
Transformer (GPT), 11

I

Intelligent, *see* Artificially
intelligent (AI)

J, K

Java Discord API (JDA), 159
Java programming, list models, 26
JavaScript Object Notation (JSON)
Chat Completion
object, 42–45
Chat structure, 33–42
DALL E model, 129–131
image endpoint, 132
list models endpoint, 27–32
moderations endpoint, 203–208

L

Legacy/deprecated models, 14
List models endpoint
Chat Endpoint
completion JSON
object, 42–45
HTTP parameters, 32
JSON object, 33–42
request creation, 32
HTTP parameters, 26
JSON response, 27

model JSON object, 27–32
ListModels.java
List models (*see* List models
endpoint)
OpenAI models, 225

M

Mobile banking
application, 178–185
Moderation models, 14
Moderations endpoint
categories, 199, 200
ContentModeratorBot.
java, 213–221
HTTP parameters, 202
intelligent discord, 222–224
JSON object, 204–208
ModerationClient.java,
208–213
offensive conversation, 222
request body, 203
structure, 203
Multimodal AI
AudioSplitter.java, 123–127
content creation, 99
DALL·E (*see* DALL·E model)
JavaCV/FFmpeg libraries, 115
splits audio files, 112–117
steps, 115
transcriptions
endpoint, 108–111
WhisperClient.java, 116–122
whisper model, 102–108

N

Natural Language Processing
    (NLP), 6
Natural Language Understanding
    (NLU), 6

O

OpenAI
    API concepts
        key, 17
    models, 225
    playground
        Add Message "+"
            symbol, 21
        API key, 17
        assistant field, 20
        chat option, 18
        identification, 18, 19
        maximum length, 22
        models, 21
        system field, 19, 20
        system role, 22, 23
        temperature, 22
        user field, 20
        view code button, 21
    REST APIs, 26
    Whisper model, 100, 102–108

P, Q

Pair-programming, 25
Podcast Visualizer, 100, 101, 139
Prompt engineering, 58

DALL·E model, 136–139
GPT-4, 126–132
text (see Text summarization)

R

REST APIs, 25

S

Slack messages, 57
    bot app, 77
        account creating, 79
        API website, 78
        app button creation, 80
        channel information, 86
        installation process, 83, 84
        OAuth/Permissions
            page, 82, 83
        scopes, 81, 82
        settings, 82
        token, 85
    channel details, 87
    ChatGPTClient.java (see
        ChatGPTClient.java)
    community management, 143
    fictional company, 65
    grab messages
        ChannelReaderSlackBot.
            java, 91–96
        convenient methods, 87
        dependencies, 87–91
        MethodsClient class, 94
    prompt engineering, 58

real world problem, 64–68
software development, 64–68
Speech recognition
system, 103–109

T, U, V

TechSupportBotDumb.
java, 160–167
TechSupportBot.java class,
178–186, 192–198
Text summarization, 68
complex conversation, 72–74
longer conversation, 71, 72
real prompt engineering, 77
suggestion information, 75–77

Too Long; Didn't Read
(tl;dr), 69, 70
Text-to-Speech (TTS) model, 12
Transcriptions endpoint, 122
HTTP parameters, 108
request body, 109–111

W, X, Y, Z

WhisperClient.java, 116–122
Whisper model, 12
AudioSplitter.java, 111
features/limitations, 105–108
meaning, 102–108
speech recognition, 102–104
transcriptions endpoint, 108–111

Printed in the United States
by Baker & Taylor Publisher Services